THE
LORTON PRISON
HIGHER EDUCATION
PROJECT

A TIME FOR ACTION

ERNESTA P. WILLIAMS, Ed.D.

WESTBOW
PRESS®
A DIVISION OF THOMAS NELSON
& ZONDERVAN

WestBow Press books may be ordered through booksellers or by contacting:

WestBow Press
A Division of Thomas Nelson & Zondervan
1663 Liberty Drive
Bloomington, IN 47403
www.westbowpress.com
1 (866) 928-1240

ISBN: 978-1-9736-0987-2 (sc)
ISBN: 978-1-9736-0989-6 (hc)
ISBN: 978-1-9736-0988-9 (e)

Library of Congress Control Number: 2017918576

Print information available on the last page.

WestBow Press rev. date: 12/20/2017

To my family, one and all, but most especially to my husband,
Dr. Samuel Williams, who has supported me
following my dreams in every way.

Contents

Acknowledgments

It was my good fortune to work at the University of the District of Columbia's (UDC) Lorton Prison College Program from 1979 to 1994. During those fifteen years, I met some remarkable individuals whose stories are the stuff of movies. This book is an attempt to memorialize a meaningful social project that touched not only their lives but mine as well. At the persistent urging of one of the participants, I embarked on this chronicle of events to shine light on a not-to-be-forgotten piece of history. This book is an attempt to give a voice to the hundreds of inmates who thought it not robbery to engage in a program of higher learning while serving time in prison.

I am indebted and grateful to all who indulged my inquisitiveness and granted interviews, both formal and informal, for this endeavor. Not only was it a labor of love, but I was able to reconnect and greet others who shared in the work. Several individuals who would have added immeasurably to this volume have passed on, but I know this effort would have had their blessings and support: Dr. Andress Taylor, Mr. Alzona Davis, Dr. Emanuel Chatman, Ms. Denise Kinlaw, and others.

Special thanks to UDC archivist Dr. Christopher Anglim, who compiled and allowed me to research the UDC archives for memorabilia that might otherwise not have been available to me. His support and assistance are appreciated. In addition to the archival materials, I had accumulated and stashed away several artifacts of my own that, from time to time, I discovered among the clutter of my home. These items have since been added to the UDC archives.

Names of the inmates that appear in this volume are real, and events are faithfully recorded. Every effort has been made to recall incidents correctly, and each person is representative of an actual participant or employee in the Lorton Prison College Program. Several years have passed since the closing of the program, and my recollections, though vivid, may be flawed somewhat. I hope you will forgive any omissions or lost perspectives that might have made valuable remembrances.

Much of this book is infused by the hard-hitting work of civil rights attorney and author Michelle Alexander whose research provides a compelling understanding of the period during which the Lorton Prison College Program flourished. In her recent book, *The New Jim Crow: Mass Incarceration in the Age of Colorblindness,* Alexander explores the social, economic, and political forces that formed the backdrop of life in America's inner cities during the period under review. After reading her book, feelings were aroused that made it uncomfortable for me not to react to the sense of racial injustice that engulfs me personally as every other African American in the nation who grapples with the issues presented. Today's social dilemmas have their origin in past policies and procedures that have now come to fruition.

Equally compelling is another work, Jaffe and Sherwood's *Dream City: the Rise and Fall of Marion Barry,* which chronicles

Washington, DC, from its inception through the early 1990s, again forming a backdrop for understanding the tensions and competing interests that shaped the capital city during this period under consideration. Together, these books give a penetrating picture, on both a macro and micro level, of how the war on drugs has affected family life, city life, and the nation as a whole.

This work is not in any way meant to condone unlawful behavior; rather, it is an attempt to shed honest light on the effects of social policies gone awry. Nor is it intended to ignore the fact that female incarceration has tripled since the 1980s, but that is another story. To all of America's black and brown pawns of the criminal justice system, this work serves as affirmation that you are worthy of a second, third, or fourth chance and that it may not have been by coincidence that you found yourself caught up in circumstances not of your own choosing and beyond your ability to control.

In 2014, a book was published entitled *College for Convicts: The Case for Higher Education in American Prisons*. In discussing state higher education prison programs around the country, the author made no mention of the Lorton Program, I suppose since DC is not a state. I accepted the fact that if this remarkable program is to be remembered, it is up to me to set the record straight.

This book should be read by educational policy makers, especially those involved in correctional education. It will be of interest to community activists and politicians as well. Higher education and grants professionals will find this work to be a valuable tool for innovation and strategic programming. For inmates, this book will demonstrate what is possibly the overarching promise of a life lived with faith and renewed hope. For young black males, it is a cautionary tale of unrealized potential. In the autobiographical words of educator and author Dr. Benjamin E. Mays, "It is conceivable, therefore, that some American youth, confused and frustrated, as I surely was, may get a glimmer of hope from reading these pages and go forth to accomplish something worthwhile in life in spite of the system" (*Born to Rebel,* preface, p. lvi).

Chapter 1

A Call to Action

The District of Columbia, or Washington, DC, has been described as the nation's capital, Chocolate City, the last colony, Dream City, the murder capital of the United States, and a host of other appellations, some positive and others quite negative. Suffice it to say that it is a not-so-typical urban city that happens to be the capital of the free world. Just sixty-nine square miles, DC is home to about six hundred thousand residents (mostly black), some of whom migrated with their parents from the Jim Crow South (North and South Carolina, primarily). There are more commuters (mostly white) doing the daily business of running a big-city government in the modern world. The residents are divided in their desire for statehood, in their search for jobs, in their ability to obtain affordable housing, and in their choice of schools. Moreover, it is a city divided by race as well as by income. One recent mayor, the Honorable Vincent Gray, ran on a platform of making DC "One City, One Future," and in the process of creating that vision, he started dramatically changing the face of Washington.

The most identifiable and celebrated part of the District of

Columbia is the federal enclave, including national monuments, government buildings, foreign embassies, parks, and statues. Washington is America's seat of government, which acts as a beacon to world travelers who flock to the city en masse throughout the year but especially in the spring and summer. Seasonally, tourists virtually take over the city streets in the downtown and nearby outlying areas. Equally ubiquitous are the commuters who arrive each day to tie up traffic from seven to six as they carry out their work responsibilities and then return to their homes in the suburbs. It is a busy town always, often to the annoyance of city residents who complain of lack of adequate parking spaces near their homes, taxation without representation (lack of home rule), and lack of a commuter tax for the interlopers. As the country's seat of government, then, Washington has its advantages, but it also has drawbacks.

For example, in terms of fiscal solvency, the Washington, DC economy has always been affected by the national fiscal climate. As the nation's capital and as a city without state status, Congress must approve the District's budgetary proposals annually, and city finances reflect the overall state of the national economy. Moreover, when the city experienced a financial crisis in the 1970s and again in the 1990s, Congress established a control board to regulate spending. As a result, the city's public college, the University of the District of Columbia, experienced a shortage of funds that led to limits on student enrollment and other cost-cutting measures. Further, the DC Crime Bill and other legislative initiatives are regularly debated and ultimately decided by the House of Representatives' subcommittee on the District. Therefore, the budget of the DC

Department of Corrections, along with other city agencies, is ultimately and directly overseen by Congress.

Like most major urban American jurisdictions of the late sixties, Washington was rife with crime, drugs, and unemployment—a bleak picture for city residents and for African American men in particular. Health indicators in the District were poor also, with high rates of homelessness, infant mortality, mental illness, drug addiction, and type 2 diabetes.

In 1968, Washington was the site of rioting in reaction to the assassination of Dr. Martin Luther King Jr. For two weeks, pent-up frustrations erupted, and there was looting and burning of downtown stores; martial law was imposed. Similar rioting took place in Watts, Newark, Cleveland, Philadelphia, Oakland, Baltimore, and Detroit. As a student at Howard University at the time, I witnessed the eerie, greenish pall that settled over the city as smoke bombs filled the air and army tanks patrolled Georgia Avenue. The urban underclass demanded jobs and an end to poverty in a nation that touted its prosperity at every turn.

The issue of public safety filled the evening news as crime rates climbed higher and higher and each year's murder rate topped the year before. Underlying the crime statistics was the prevalence of drugs in the cities, notably marijuana, heroin, and cocaine. Marijuana, the drug of choice among the inner-city youth, was illegal and resulted in felony convictions for possession, distribution, and trafficking. Thus, as early as 1970, reports were confirming that the number of black men in prison (236,000) had surpassed the number of black men in college (227,000). The reports actually exacerbated misuse of the data. While it may have been true that more black men

3

were under the jurisdiction of corrections (including prison, parole, and probation) than in college, in most instances indeterminate prison sentences were being compared with a more restricted time in college, usually four to seven years. Thus, at any given time, the same men were being kept in prison as the college men were being rotated, thereby creating a faulty comparison.

Continuing the war on drugs declared by President Richard Nixon in 1971, President Ronald Reagan implemented strict policies in 1982 that were intended to curb the use and prevalence of these substances; however, these policies further depressed neighborhoods and individual citizens. Then crack cocaine hit the streets in 1985, becoming the scourge of the inner city as it provided a cheap high and was readily available (Alexander 2010, 50–51).

The thrust of the war on drugs was especially evident in the inner cities where drugs were plentiful. Law enforcement targeted low-income areas, using special tactics to ferret out those involved in the drug trade; the courts supported the effort with harsher sentences that were given out for the cheaper crack cocaine (which most blacks used) as opposed to the more expensive powder cocaine (which whites could afford). As a result, "punitive 'zero tolerance policies' ... effectively funnel[led] youth of color from schools to jail" (Alexander, 11). In turn, stringent laws were enacted in 1988 with mandatory sentencing, which had the effect of incarcerating a large percentage of the black men and boys of the city. Even the schools began to implement tougher sanctions for misbehavior in the interest of public safety and joined with law enforcement to extract those students considered to be "undesirable."

Urban communities also experienced a decided rise of unemployment and female-headed households, and there was a high truancy rate among black boys. As Mead explains:

> The decline in employment [was] especially great among black men, a principal reason why poverty today is much higher among blacks than whites. In 1960, 83 percent of both white and black men were working or looking for work. By 1988, the white rate had dropped to 77 percent, the black rate to 71 percent. Black unemployment rates, which typically run twice those for whites, reached 20 percent during the 1980s, and among black male teenagers an astounding 49 percent. (1992, 10)

This urban underclass continues to predominate in cities across America where blacks and Latinos tend to reside.

This dichotomy was further spelled out in the wide academic achievement gap between white and black students, which has been observed for the past thirty years. Various approaches have been tried to fix the problem of underachieving poor (mostly black and Latino) students, including Head Start and free lunch programs, charter schools, merit pay for teachers, and higher standards in general. When the statistics are examined, race seems to be the deciding factor of who succeeds in this society. David Kipp noted a College Board study that reported the following:

> Black male students are 2.4 times as likely to have been suspended and twice as likely to have repeated

a grade as white males. High-school graduation rates tell the same story—just 42% of black males graduated on time in 2006, compared with 71% of white males. After leaving school, these dropouts generally seem to encounter only more failure: Among 16- to 24-year-old black men not enrolled in school, fewer than half have jobs; about a third are in prison or jail, or on probation or parole. (2010, 1)

Today, the public schools of Washington, DC, have the widest racial achievement gap in the nation (Kipp 2010).

Moreover, a national state of emergency has emerged called a "school-to-prison pipeline." Sociologist Nancy Heitzeg, in a book so-named, describes the "growing pattern of tracking students out of educational institutions directly and/or indirectly into the juvenile and adult criminal justice systems via suspension/ expulsion and increasingly arrest for minor infractions" (2016, 7). Where schools adopt zero-tolerance disciplinary policies, funding for regular school resources must also include surveillance cameras, security guards, and metal detectors. Between the ages of twelve and seventeen, boys of color in the nation's capital and other inner cities are being pushed out of the classroom as a result of punitive and stringent disciplinary practices that feed the correctional system with an ever-present labor pool. Once suspended or expelled from school, grades are failed, drop out or stop out occurs, and a crime-filled life on the streets results. These youngsters are left to feel shame, fear, and uselessness. Two black psychiatrists, William Grier and Price Cobbs (1968), wrote a book entitled *Black Rage* in which they attempt to explain the cause of this pent-up rage. They note:

> As boys approach adulthood, masculinity becomes more and more bound up with money making. In a capitalistic society economic wealth is inextricably interwoven with manhood ... The ultimate power is the freedom to understand and alter one's life. It is this power, both individually and collectively, which has been denied the black man. (50)

In America today, by the time black boys reach adulthood (eighteen), too many are already well acquainted with the justice system. Many have dropped out of high school; some have fathered children. "Those who do not drop out may find that their discipline and juvenile or criminal records haunt them when they apply to college or for a scholarship or government grant, or try to enlist in the military or find employment" (Heitzeg 2016, 11). In addition, without the foundation of at least a high school education, the few jobs that are available pay minimum wages that cannot adequately support an average-sized family of four. So a life of crime becomes appealing.

Gentrification has also played a role. As more and more DC neighborhoods are redeveloped, low-income housing has become harder and harder to find in the District, and long-time residents are having to move to the suburbs where rent is cheaper. Others see some of the development as long overdue remodeling as a result of the riots of the sixties. In any case, the city is experiencing unprecedented growth and urban renewal. In every quadrant of the city, construction sites dominate the landscape, yet even these jobs are filled primarily by out-of-town contracting companies. With all of the influx of new businesses, new apartments and condos, coupled with reduced mileage to worksites, urban living in DC has become quite fashionable for those who can afford the new higher living costs. The majority of the District's African Americans, however, reside in Wards 7 and 8 where households are densely populated and incomes below the poverty level predominate.

Health disparities continue to be prevalent among the District's African American population as well. A Georgetown University report found that infant mortality and homicide rates continue to be high, with a life expectancy almost fifteen years less than for whites. Moreover, high levels of obesity, smoking, coronary heart disease, diabetes, prostate cancer, and stroke disproportionately affect African American residents (Jackson 2016).

Today, these types of urban social and economic disparities have compounded and are reflected in the much higher percentage of African Americans incarcerated in the United States in proportion to the population. In fact, it has been noted that "The U.S. has less than five percent of the world's population, yet we incarcerate about a quarter of its prisoners—some 2.2 million people" (Sanders, 2015), and these are disproportionately black or Hispanic. The current plight is summarized by Alexander: "In major cities across the United States, the majority of young black men are under the control of the criminal justice system or saddled with criminal records" (p. 164). As recent as 2011 in Washington, DC, it has been estimated that 95 percent of African American men have been involved in the criminal justice system at some point in their lives (Drucker, p. 45). Such statistics, which Karpowitz (2017) calls "structural inequality," underscore what is obvious to many: the racial divide continues to be the unacknowledged elephant in the room in American society.

References

Alexander, M. 2010. *The New Jim Crow: Mass Incarceration in the Age of Colorblindness*. New York: The New Press.

Drucker, E. 2011. *A Plague of Prisons: The Epidemiology of Mass Incarceration in America*. New York: The New Press.

Grier, W.H. and Cobbs, P.M. 1968. *Black Rage*. New York: Basic Books, Inc.

Heitzeg, N.A. 2016. *The School-to-Prison Pipeline: Education, Discipline, and Racialized Double Standards*. Santa Barbara: Praeger.

Jackson, M. 2016. *The Health of the African-American Community in the District of Columbia: Disparities And Recommendations*. Washington: Georgetown University.

Karpowitz, D. *College in Prison: Reading in the Age of Mass Incarceration*. New Brunswick, NJ: Rutgers University Press.

Kipp, D.L. Fall 2010. "The Widest Achievement Gap." *National Affairs* 5.

Mead, L.M. 1992. *The New Politics of Poverty*. New York: Basic Books, Inc.

Sanders, B. 2015. "We Must End For-Profit Prisons." Retrieved from http://www.huffingtonpost.com/bernie-sanders/we-must-end-for-profit-pr_b.

Chapter 2

A Historical Overview

The Lorton Reformatory was built in Lorton, Virginia (Fairfax County) in 1910 to house sixty of the District's miscreants and, later, inmates convicted of felony (federal) crimes. President Theodore Roosevelt commissioned the prison as a model of Progressive Era correctional facilities that would rehabilitate inmates through the discipline of hard work. As described, "Lorton originally had no fences or bars. Its classical-revival architecture, arch-lined walkways, and open dormitories instead of cells made it look more like a college campus than a place of penitence" (Shin 2001). The vast tract of land north of the Occoquan River covered over a thousand acres and eventually included a dairy, orchards, and farm crops cultivated by the inmates themselves. It featured, additionally, both industrial and trade instruction. In fact, many of the later brick buildings on the property were actually built by the inmates who learned masonry and carpentry on site.

Over time, the facilities expanded to cover over three thousand acres and were renamed the Lorton Correctional Complex, consisting of a group of correctional facilities located about twenty miles from the District of Columbia: Youth Centers I and II; the Minimum Security Facility at Occoquan; Central Facility (medium security); and "Big Lorton," as the maximum security facility was called. The Lorton Complex was the only prison in the United States that housed all classes of male inmates. (The District's female offenders originally were sent to prison in Alderson, West Virginia, and only in later years were some transported to Lorton.) By the 1970s, the inmate population at Lorton had reached four thousand, and politicians were being approached regarding unrest and escapes; the answer was to erect chain-link fences around each facility, fences that became even stronger in the 1980s and 1990s: "Officials replaced the old wire with coils of stainless-steel and aluminum long-blade razor wire—also called concertina wire— with 2-inch-wide blades on each side" (Shin 2001). These efforts temporarily appeased the Virginia residents in the surrounding area and kept them safely separated from the District's violent criminal element in their midst.

However, in many respects, Lorton was an extension of the larger DC community. Inmate and radio personality Petey Greene was allowed to broadcast his show from Lorton, and the father of go-go music, Chuck Brown, was also an inmate there. Convicted White House conspirator G. Gordon Liddy occupied a cell at Lorton in the fallout of the Watergate conspiracy and the impeachment of President Richard Nixon. So the men at Lorton were reflective of the larger community and were fully knowledgeable about the issues and challenges facing their loved ones.

Central Facility was the locus for the Lorton Project or, as it more formally came to be known, the Lorton Prison College

Program (LPCP). This medium-security section was similar to a campus setting in that the inmates were housed dormitory style rather than in cellblocks. It featured a colonial style courtyard with an open-air design. The Administration Building and the warden's office were located at Central amid sprawling lawns of greenery and quiet. There was a large chapel with a life-sized crucifix as well as a cafeteria, various industries, a gymnasium, basketball hoops, and a TV room. The real reminder of the prison setting was the central guard tower through which everyone entered the premises via steel doors that buzzed when opened. At this point, each visitor was frisked and subjected to a full body scan.

Brief History of Prisons in the United States

Since the opening of the first penitentiary in the United States in Philadelphia in 1790, the Walnut Street Jail, efforts have been underway to deal with crime in America. It was early believed that through hard work, humane treatment, and Bible reading, prisoners could be reformed (Edge 2009). Through trial and error, prisons opened in various states, each employing a slightly different methodology to change behavior. For example, Auburn Prison, which opened in New York in 1821, relied on silence, separation, and hard labor to create discipline. Solitary confinement and whippings were used to maintain order. Prisoners, male and female, had to keep their eyes down and march in lockstep to meals and had no communication with the outside world (Edge).

After the Civil War (1861–1865), which left the South with damaged crops and burned property, the freed slaves and others fled to the urban slums of the North in such large numbers that there were not enough jobs to absorb the unskilled workers. As a result of joblessness and poverty, crime increased, and the prisons became overcrowded, violent, and disease ridden (Edge). New methods of prison management were needed, and new practices emerged. Chain gangs with prisoners wearing identifiable striped clothing and harsh treatment followed. Despite the passage of the Fourteenth Amendment in 1868, which promised all citizens equal treatment under the law, in the South racial disparities or black codes were rampant, and African Americans were punished severely and kept in filthy prison conditions for violation of what became known as Jim Crow laws. Laws against vagrancy and improper gestures toward whites were vigorously enforced against blacks, and under violation of these rules, prisoners became slaves of the state and could be hired out to vicious employers to work off their sentences (Alexander 2010).

In the late nineteenth century, various reformers came on the scene emphasizing education and training (Esperian 2010). In 1870, the National Prison Congress, made up of representatives of twenty-four states, met to consider prison reforms. The result of this commission was the idea of the indeterminate sentence and the principle of parole, which would allow an inmate to earn his way out of prison through good behavior. Elmira Prison in New York adopted this model and also included physical education and self-sufficiency in its programming. The reform movement also resulted in women prisoners and youth offenders being housed separate from the men (Edge).

The Progressive Era of prison reform (1900–1920) saw

the emergence of the scientific approach to the crime issue. Criminologists began to see the offender as an individual who could be treated and cured of antisocial behavior. Various laws were passed in an effort to eliminate prostitution, drug addiction, and alcoholism. Psychologists were hired to classify the prisoners according to the likelihood of their recidivism. Others thought prisons were inherently bad and ineffective and that new methods of achieving public safety should be found (Edge).

At the same time, lynching of black male citizens was at an all-time high in the South. The so-called Red Summer of 1921 was a time of civil unrest with white mobs openly attacking and killing black men. The resulting lynching and shootings were spurred by the cadre of black men returning from World War I looking for respect and jobs after having fought for freedom abroad. Finding neither, labor conflicts and racial tension increased between the races, and riots broke out in several cities across the United States, including Washington, DC; Chicago, Illinois; Elaine, Arkansas; Tulsa, Oklahoma and elsewhere.

By the 1930s, crime was recognized as a national problem of major proportions. The country was in the throes of the Depression, and unemployment was high. Unions protested the right of inmates to make goods for sale in another state, and Congress passed the Hawes-Cooper Act to make it illegal. President Herbert Hoover formed a group led by George Wickersham to study the entire criminal justice system. The group produced a fourteen-volume report, which concluded that the current prison system "does not reform the criminal" and equally does not "protect society." Moreover, "[T]here is reason to believe that it contributes to the increase of crime by hardening the prisoner" (Edge, p. 44–45). One result of the report was separation of prisoners into minimum or maximum-secured facilities according to the severity of their crime(s) or other criteria such as length of sentence.

The Federal Bureau of Prisons was formed in 1930 to oversee the large increase in federal prisons and prisoners. Federal prisons such as Alcatraz (California), Attica (New York), Folsom (New York), and San Quentin (California) were inhabited by violent gangs of the worst prisoners. These facilities were dangerous, overcrowded, and the site of prison rioting by inmates disgruntled about their living conditions.

After World War II (1941–1945), J. Edgar Hoover expanded the focus of the Federal Bureau of Investigation (FBI) to crack down on domestic organized crime by such groups as the Mafia. The FBI's "Ten Most Wanted" criminals list was started, and several infamous figures were captured and imprisoned.

By the early 1950s, emphasis was being placed on changing the inmates' attitudes and behavior. The American Prison Association changed its name to the American Correctional Association, and prison guards began to be called correctional officers. More mental health workers were hired to place emphasis on rehabilitation through step-by-step programming offering rewards and punishment. More prisons were being built with windows, libraries, and athletic equipment.

Then in 1955 the case of Emmett Till in Mississippi proved the unfairness of the American system of criminal justice. A fourteen-year-old African American youngster, visiting in the South, was beaten, shot to death, and his mutilated body thrown into the

Tallahatchie River for whistling at a white woman. An all-white jury of men found the woman's husband and half brother innocent of the murder, but a few months later, the men confessed. The crime and trial caused the civil rights community, led by Rev. Dr. Martin Luther King Jr., and the Nation of Islam, an African American separatist Muslim group led by ex-offender Malcolm X and others, to protest. The two leaders had different ideologies and separate followers, but both expressed pent-up frustration with the unfair treatment and marginalization of black Americans.

Subsequently, the decade of the 1960s sparked a prisoner rights movement that forced another reconsideration of crime and punishment in America. Social upheavals over the Vietnam War and the deaths of President John F. Kennedy, Malcolm X, Rev. Dr. Martin Luther King Jr., and Attorney General Robert Kennedy, all of whom were senselessly gunned down, brought the issues to the forefront. The Supreme Court upheld a prisoner's right to protection under the Constitution. All forms of corporal punishment were outlawed, and prison conditions had to meet basic standards of decency. In 1965, President Lyndon Johnson established the President's Crime Commission to again look at the entire criminal justice system and make recommendations for improvement in preparing the prisoners for their eventual life on the outside. Treatment programs, halfway houses, educational programs, professional counseling, and other progressive ideas were instituted across the nation. Colleges and universities began to offer degree programs not only for the inmates but also for criminal justice majors to improve the training of prison workers. More criminal justice degree programs were started to develop highly trained professionals in the field of corrections.

Emphasis began being placed on the environmental factors that breed crime.

Others citizens felt that the system as a whole and individual judges in particular were too lenient; they favored a get-tough policy. In the 1970s, tougher sentencing laws were instituted, which gave each crime a fixed-length prison term, requiring judges to limit their discretion at sentencing. Three-strike laws were enforced for repeat offenders, and the prisons began to swell. From 1973 to 1997, the US inmate population grew by more than 500 percent (Edge). As the PEW study confirms,

> ... the growth flowed primarily from changes in sentencing laws, inmate release decisions, community supervision practices and other correctional policies that determine who goes to prison and for how long. (p. 6)

Add to this picture the rise of the prison industrial complex, a system of supply and demand that sought to privatize the prison industry. The 1970s saw the growth of the prison industrial complex as more prisons were built and more men were added to the prison population in response to policies and practices of what began as a war on drugs.

The War on Drugs

Central to the problem of incarceration of black and brown men has been the war on drugs, formally begun in 1982 under the administration of President Ronald Reagan. In 1981, Congress passed the Military Cooperation with Law Enforcement Act. As a result, the drug war has been waged using Special Weapons and Tactics (SWAT) teams that operate as paramilitary agencies of law enforcement in all of the major cities. Armed SWAT teams have exercised raids on homes, projects, and even schools in search of drugs. Money, equipment, and weapons are given to local police departments in support of the war efforts, and with more drug arrests and seizures of assets, more federal grants have been awarded to jurisdictions. As Alexander (2010) notes, "Although the majority of illegal drug users and dealers nationwide are white, three-fourths of all people imprisoned for drug offenses have been black or Latino" (p. 97).

Immigration issues have confounded the problem even further as drug cartels move from country to country distributing their wares, especially from South America into North America. There is a multitude of conduits stretching from Mexico and Colombia through underground tunnels, border breaches, and smuggling operations, all designed to filter drugs into this country. Along with the drugs, illegal aliens (primarily Latinos) have "invaded" the country by the millions, adding to the underclass population and vying for jobs and educational opportunities (Alexander).

Individuals have made billions of dollars off the lucrative business of sale and distribution of drugs. For inner-city residents with few options for upward mobility, the temptation of the drug trade money seems like an easy way to escape an impoverished environment. Too often, however, drug trade results in drug use and more criminal activity, making those who participate susceptible to arrest. As the founder of the LPCP declared, "Many of the best men in the community end up in jail, because the number of things a black man can do that are considered against the law are so great."

What started as a well-funded attempt to rid the inner cities of crack cocaine was a not-so-well disguised plan of attack on the black and brown male population. In 1986, the Anti-Drug Abuse Act was passed, which included mandatory minimum sentences for distributors of cocaine, a powerful hallucinogen. However, there was a "far more severe punishment for distribution of crack— associated with blacks—than powder cocaine, associated with whites" (Alexander, p. 52). This harsh sentence, as much as five years in prison, was applied to first-time offenders in possession of the substance base, the severest penalty in the federal system, according to Alexander. In summary, "... while Blacks represent only about 13% of the drug users nationally, Black people represent 38% of those arrested for drug offenses, and of that number 55% of those convicted of drug offenses, and 74% of those sent to prison" (Herzing).

Heitzeg (2016) has noted that the juvenile justice system is also extending its reach as schools have become more punitive in policies governing truancy, insubordination, disorderly conduct, and other actions once considered minor infractions. She notes that "Black students are suspended and expelled at three times the rate of their white peers" (p. 66). Schools have begun to support the "pipeline" by adopting such policies and nomenclature as metal detectors, drug searches, lockdowns, gang databases, and police presence. Now students as young as eight or ten face the possibility of not only suspension and expulsion but referral to adult courts, actions that lead to even more serious infractions of rules and harsher consequences. In fact, "Youth who have encounters with juvenile justice, especially those who have been incarcerated, are less likely to return to school and more likely to be imprisoned as adults" (Heitzeg, p. 65). The zero-tolerance approach to crime has extended itself into the school system.

Today, America's prison population is soaring at over two million—the highest incarcerated population in the world (PEW 2010, Esperian 2010, Lagemann 2016). Alexander notes: "The impact of the drug war has been astounding. In less than thirty years, the U.S. penal population exploded from around 300,000 to more than 2 million, with drug convictions accounting for the majority of the increase" (p. 6). Many of these individuals were and are repeat offenders, and some of these are serving time for nonviolent drug or property offenses. All of the social ills described are reflected in the much higher percentage of African American inmates in the United States in proportion to the population. As the PEW study confirms, "Simply stated, incarceration in America is concentrated among African American men" (p. 6). In a sixty-nine-square-mile city such as Washington, DC, these issues are magnified and stark. And Drucker (2011) reveals, "… in Washington, D.C., more than 95 percent of African American men have been in prison in their lifetimes" (p. 45). Such a startling fact forces any reasonable person to ask, what's wrong with this picture? The war on drugs has been fought so vigorously that our prisons are bursting at the seams and more prisons are being built every day.

The prison industrial complex (PIC) is a term used to describe what has become big business, employing thousands of individuals and forming the core of area economies. For example, the

Correctional Corporation of America (CCA), headquartered in Nashville, Tennessee, was formed in 1983 to privatize the prison industry. In partnership with the government, CCA began to build, buy, expand, and manage state and federal prison facilities at a fast pace as a full-service provider of correctional services, including inmate transportation. As the leader in the private corrections market today, CCA runs more than seventy facilities and houses upwards of ninety thousand inmates across the country. More significant, since 1994, CCA has been a member of the New York Stock Exchange.

Prison management has indeed become a lucrative and growing enterprise, and CCA, along with the GEO Group, dominates the industry. According to a study prepared by the Justice Policy Institute (2011):

> Due to ineffective criminal justice policies that promote incarceration over more effective alternatives, an increasing need for prison beds has resulted in more private prison contracts and subsequently more revenue for private prison companies as states have less money to pay for the construction of their own prison beds. As a result of this increasing trend of incarceration, private prison companies have seen exponential growth in revenues, benefitting greatly from more people being placed behind bars. (p. 9)

The study revealed that these two largest private prison companies (CCA and the GEO Group) grossed $2.9 billion in revenue in 2010 alone and spent millions lobbying and strategically distributing political campaign contributions to candidates and causes in support of self-serving policies. There is an economic incentive for keeping prison occupation at a high level.

The study showed, further, the connection between high government officials and those leading the private prison conglomerates. Political influence by former lobbyists presents major conflicts of interest, which serve to keep the prison industry afloat.

In addition to the PIC, the media does its part to perpetuate negative stereotypes of young black and brown males as predators. Great strides have been made for more inclusion of minorities in entertainment through television and movie roles; however, reality-based news disproportionately features black males as aggressive, violent criminals (Watkins 1998). Some hip-hop music lyrics and other popular culture misrepresent African Americans as misogynistic, hedonistic, and money-grabbing ne'er-do-wells.

Even more disturbing, prison growth is being predicted based upon fourth-grade reading scores, recognizing the strong predictive nexus between lack of education and crime. The 2007 and 2008 National Assessment of Educational Progress (NAEP) math and reading scores for District of Columbia fourth graders was the lowest in the nation (Kipp, p. 6).

References

Alexander, M. 2010. *The New Jim Crow: Mass Incarceration in the Age of Colorblindness*. New York: The New Press.

Drucker, E. 2011. *A Plague of Prisons: The Epidemiology of Mass Incarceration in America*. New York: The New Press.

Edge, L.B. 2009. *Locked Up: A History of the U.S. Prison System*. Minneapolis: Twenty-First Century Books.

Esperian, J.H. December 2010. "The Effect of Prison Education Programs on Recidivism." *The Journal of Correctional Education* 61 (4): 316–334.

Heitzeg, N.A. 1916. *The School-to-Prison Pipeline: Education, Discipline, and the Racialized Double Standards*. Santa Barbara: Praeger.

Herzing, R. "What Is the Prison Industrial Complex?" http://www.publiceye.org/defendingjustice/overview/herzing_pic.html.

Justice Policy Institute. June 2011. *Gaming the System: How the Political Strategies of Private Prison Companies Promote Ineffective Incarceration Policies*. Washington, DC.

Kipp, D.L. Fall 2010. "The Widest Achievement Gap." *National Affairs* 5.

Lagemann, E.C. 2016. *Liberating Minds: The Case for College in Prison*. New York: The New Press.

Shin, A. 2001. *"Ten Things to Do before Closing a Prison."* March 9. http://www.washingtoncitypaper.com/articles/21385/ten-things-to-do-before-closing-a-prison.

The PEW Charitable Trusts. 2010. *Collateral Costs: Incarceration's Effect on Economic Mobility.* Washington, DC: The PEW Charitable Trusts.

Chapter 3

From Slavery to Incarceration

Black males, in particular, have always posed a problem in this country—since the days of slavery when they were considered three-fifths human, were not allowed to read or write, and were controlled by paddyrollers who practiced intimidation and harsh physical punishment. The "menace" of the uneducated black man continued post-slavery and was a cause for fear; Jim Crow laws suppressing the black vote, interracial marriage, and other civil liberties were strictly enforced to keep the black man "in check." Michele Alexander (2010), in her eye-opening book, *The New Jim Crow: Mass Incarceration,* discusses how the prison conglomerates today have replaced the Jim Crow laws or black codes of the South, being equally effective in keeping black men locked away, out of the political, economic, and social structure of this nation. We have progressed from the terrorism of slavery, through Jim Crow and now mass incarceration. The result is the same: black male suppression.

No one knows the extent of the lasting psychological trauma of slavery, yet denial of education has long been recognized as key to breaking the chains of oppression. For this reason, education has been touted in minority communities as the pathway to middle class acceptance in American society. Consequently, public education at every level is available for those who seek it. But beyond free public secondary education, it is considered a privilege by many Americans to enroll in higher education. In fact, for centuries, discussions in this country have traditionally centered around the question, is higher education a privilege or a right? Those who consider higher education a privilege argue that only the best and brightest should be admitted to college and that college is not for everyone.

For the urban underclass caught in the vicious cycle of crime-arrest-incarceration, some of those best and brightest have turned to negative behaviors that accommodate their uneducated intellects. What happens to an intelligent child who sees no way out of his ghetto circumstances? Too often, without serious or prolonged intervention, he/she grows up adopting the behavior and lifestyles of those around him/her and makes choices that lead to their residence in penitentiaries, behind lock and key. With no positive role models, they learn to adapt to the negative ones—the dope dealers, drug users, and gang bangers.

But this approach to the issue is based on a deficit model that emphasizes the black man as a problem to be solved rather than a valued human being to be encouraged and developed (Harper 2012). Toldson and Johns (2016) discuss the need for a perspective that erases the deficit model in favor of one that examines the resilience of black males to overcome their environment and the need for studies based on more accurate data. Equally important are the opportunities available to the younger cohorts of black males being schooled, some feel, largely by white female teachers who have little or no empathy for their minority male students (Warren 2016).

Every federal prison is mandated by law to have a general services library and to provide opportunity for inmates without a high school diploma to pursue the general education diploma or GED (Zoukis 2014). The case for prisoner education really rests on getting the biggest return on investment. This value-added approach argues that it is much cheaper to invest in education for an inmate than it is to house a prisoner multiple times during his lifetime. Vocational programs are offered as well, leading to certification in a marketable skill. With education and training, the argument goes, the individual will be more employable upon release. Conversely, without an education and marketable skills, most prisoners will recidivate. There is general consensus on this value-added approach.

However, when we add to the discussion the question of whether inmates should be afforded a *college* education, the sparks really fly. But, some argue, *higher* education is a different situation. Critics ask, why should someone who has violated the laws of society have access to higher education when law-abiding taxpayers cannot afford to send their own children to college? Charges of coddling the inmates reflect the desire to punish, not rehabilitate.

On the other hand, some consider higher education a right, especially in a nation such as the United States, which is dependent on higher thinking and training for the advancements that keep us ahead as a world power. Those who consider higher education a right argue that it is in the interest of public safety and progress to educate the entire citizenry since we cannot predict who will be of benefit to society. Even prisoners, they argue, who one day will return to society, should be educated. Do we want them to be productive and reformed citizens or continue, without education, to prey on others? Even some prison administrators support the idea of college programs for inmates due to the inmate's lower recidivism rates once released and "for their ability to help manage [other] prisoners" (Pfeiffer 2000).

Philosophically, the larger question becomes, can the United States afford to disenfranchise and marginalize a disproportionately significant segment of the African American and growing Latino population? The damage done to the men themselves, their families, their communities, and the nation is inestimable, leading 2016 presidential candidate Bernie Sanders to call this state of mass incarceration a "major human tragedy" (2015).

Drucker (2011), in his work *A Plague of Prisons,* agrees with Alexander and Sanders and claims that mass incarceration has reached epidemic proportions in America. He refers to the "'collateral damage' of mass incarceration: the children, grandchildren, wives, parents, siblings, and other family members of those incarcerated over the course of the last thirty-five years" (p. 44). This damage is reflected today in higher instances of domestic violence, child abuse, truancy, unemployment, homelessness, infant mortality, and juvenile crime.

Prison Higher Education Programs

History shows us that several notable modern-day writers and thinkers have emerged from the prison experience. Many used their time behind bars to cultivate their minds and worldview.

Malcolm X studied the dictionary and the Koran, becoming a national spokesman for American followers of Islam. Nelson Mandela emerged from prison to become the president of South Africa. Dr. Martin Luther King Jr. wrote the powerful *Letter from a Birmingham Jail* while incarcerated. Dr. Randall Horton became a noted poet and professor of creative writing at a major university. Other inspirational prisoners who made valuable contributions to America and the world include Russian writers Fyodor Dostoyevsky and Salman Rushdie, as well as Leo Tolstoy, Miguel de Cervantes, and Oscar Wilde, to name a few. Reading and writing become strong modes for both reflection and expression behind bars.

Prison higher education programs, thus, have been debated vigorously through the years. Usually the subject is posed as an economic issue. In times of austerity, it becomes a convenient scapegoat to cut out all prisoner privileges. However, studies have shown the high correlation between illiteracy and crime, between education and employment, and between unemployment and crime (PEW 2010). This triangulation suggests, and studies show, that postsecondary educational opportunity for inmates leads to greater employment, reduced crime, and lower recidivism. Furthermore, the research shows that the cost to provide one year of in-state college tuition is much cheaper than providing one year of incarceration, the average to incarcerate being upward of $25,000. In fact, "Statistics have indicated that the cost of keeping a prisoner in prison for one year exceeds the cost of educating prisoners for one year by a 10 to 1 ratio" (Granoff 2005).

Prison college programs, therefore, were seen by many in the early 1970s and mideighties as a means of encouraging good behavior, changing lives, and reducing recidivism. Variations on the theme sprang up all over the country in the form of special classes, degree programs, correspondence classes and other arrangements. In 1982 alone, there were about 350 postsecondary prison programs operating in most states across the country (Zoukis 2014). Associate and baccalaureate degree programs were offered by the University of the District of Columbia, Boston University, Marist College, Syracuse University, Patten University, Cornell University, Bard College, Georgetown University, and others. Several colleges donated books to prisons to support their libraries and in-prison higher education programs. It was generally known and acknowledged that these programs worked.

The issue of Pell Grants for prisoners, however, was and continues to be a special bone of contention. Title IV of the Higher Education Act of 1965 and subsequent amendments authorized payment to low-income individuals to ensure access to a college education by making it more affordable. Senator Claiborne Pell (D-RI) led the fight in Congress to extend the funding to prisoners, which was granted in 1972 as Basic Educational Opportunity Grants. In recognition of his strong advocacy, the grants were named for him in 1980 (Anderson 2013). But conservative congressional legislators from Senator Jesse Helms (R-NC) to Senator Kay Bailey Hutchinson (R-TX) have fought vigorously to deny the grants to prisoners. Pell himself defended the need-based program against its critics:

> The Pell Grant program functions as a quasi-entitlement. A student qualifies for a grant, and

the size of the grant depends on the availability of appropriations. Thus, the child of a police officer would not be denied a grant in favor of a prisoner. If both are eligible, both receive grants. (J.M. Taylor, p. 55)

By 1993, there were estimated to be 38,000 prisoners in college programs throughout the country (Lillis 1994). Of this number, approximately 80 percent were receiving Pell Grants (Sarri 1993). Such a statistic at face value may seem excessive. At the height of the practice, however, less than 1 percent of the $4.7 million Pell Grant disbursements went to prison inmates, and the average amount they received was merely $1,400 (J.M. Taylor, *Straight Low*, p. 55). Even this amount went to Corrections to offer the program, not directly to the inmates themselves. Yet, after years of debate on the congressional floor, in 1994, subsequent to a 312 to 116 vote in the House of Representatives, President William Jefferson "Bill" Clinton signed the National Crime Bill, the law that eliminated all Pell Grant disbursements to state or federal prisoners. Marc Mauer, executive director of the Sentencing Project, a criminal justice advocacy group, commented: "We know that the prohibition that Congress placed on Pell grants (to prisoners) had nothing to do with research, nothing to do with financial priorities, and everything to do with politics" (Abdul-Alim 2001). Today, Dallas Pell of New York continues her father's advocacy on this issue.

The Higher Education Act of 1998 further limited financial aid by denying Pell eligibility to those convicted for drug possession or trafficking as well, virtually calling a halt to most prison higher education programs since a disproportionately high number of inmates were in prison on drug convictions. So we might consider from about 1970 to 1997 the heyday for the proliferation of college programs for prisoners. But certainly, by 2002, there was a virtual end of college programs behind bars, and only in the past few years has the opportunity begun to reemerge.

Consequently, in Washington, DC, in 1968, perhaps more dramatically than in any place else in the country, the setting was ripe for a radical, innovative approach to extricate from the system the District's lost manpower. The Lorton Project was envisioned as a desert oasis, an eye in the midst of a raging and growing storm.

References

Abdul-Alim, J. October 2011. "Panelists Agree Compelling Evidence Needed to Make Case for Incarcerated Individuals to Regain Eligibility For Pell Grant." *Diverse Education.* Retrieved from http://diverseeducation.com/cache/print.php?articleId=16471.

Alexander, M. 2010. *The New Jim Crow: Mass Incarceration in the Age of Colorblindness.* New York: The New Press.

Anderson, N., 2013. "Push to Give Pell Grants to Prisoners." *Washington Post,* B3, December 9.

Granoff, G. May 2005. "Prison College Programs Unlock the Keys to Human Potential, *Education Update Online.* Retrieved from http://www.educationupdate.com/archives/2005/May/html/FEAT-BehindBars.html.

Lillis, I. March 1994. "Prison Education Programs Reduced." *Correctional Compendium* 19 (3): 1–4.

Pfeiffer, M.B. November 2000. "Inmate College Programs Now Rare. *Poughkeepsie Journal.* Retrieved from http:/www.poughkeepsiejournal.com/projects/prison/po111700sl.shtml.

Sanders, B. 2015. "We Must End For-Profit Prisons." Retrieved from http://www.huffingtonpost.com/bernie-sanders/we-must-end-for-profit-pr_b.

Sarri, R. 1993. "Educational Programs in the State Department of Corrections: A Survey of the States." Paper presented at the American Society of Criminology, Phoenix, AZ (November).

Taylor, J.M. 2008. "Pell Grants for Prisoners: Why Should We Care? *Straight Low* 9 (2).

The PEW Charitable Trusts. 2010. *Collateral Costs: Incarceration's Effect on Economic Mobility.* Washington, DC: The PEW Charitable Trusts.

Toldson, I.A. and Johns, D.J. June 1916. "Erasing Deficits." *Teachers College Record* 118: 1–7.

Zoukis, C. 2014. *College for Convicts: The Case for Higher Education in American Prisons.* Jefferson, NC: McFarland & Company, Inc.

Chapter 4

Changing Lanes

The Lorton Project began in 1969 at Federal City College, "the nation's first Urban Land Grant institution with a strong commitment to educational innovation and community involvement" (Taylor, A. 1974). Planning had begun in 1968, and the idea of an academic program in Lorton Prison was conceived as a joint effort between then Federal City College and the District of Columbia Department of Corrections. James Freeman, John H. Johnson, and William Jefferson of the DC Department of Corrections and Andress Taylor, dean of experimental programs at Federal City College, began talking about a prison college program when they realized that existing programs were not meeting the needs of highly motivated inmates at the Lorton Complex. The project was planned and initiated by Federal City College's Department of Experimental Programs where Taylor was the dean; Gene Emanuel was the program's first on-site coordinator. Later, in 1977, when Federal City College merged with Miner Teachers College and Washington Technical Institute to become the University of the District of Columbia (UDC), founder Andress Taylor returned to the classroom as a full professor in the UDC English Studies Department. The Prison College Program was then placed in the Division of Continuing Education under the leadership of Dr. Irvin D. Gordy, dean, and Alzona J. Davis, former Columbia University lecturer in economics, was hired as project director.

The University of the District of Columbia is the nation's only urban, land-grant, historically black institution. Its institutional roots date back to 1851 when a white abolitionist, Myrtilla Miner, founded a School for Girls. It is also the only public institution of higher education in the nation's capital and sits among several prestigious and well-endowed private institutions: Howard University, George Washington University, Catholic University, American University, Gallaudet University, Georgetown University, and Trinity Washington University. In this respect, DC is also a college town—attracting motivated and highly educated professionals who compete for jobs and other city resources. UDC's current mission is to educate citizens of the District and the world at all levels of postsecondary educational engagement and workforce development. The Lorton Project enabled UDC to meet its land grant mission in dramatic fashion.

Conceptually, the Lorton Project was an ambitious undertaking in response to inmate unrest. The men had complained of being warehoused with long sentences and nothing to do to change their circumstances upon release. Frequent disturbances occurred among the nearly 100 percent black inmate population at Lorton under the authority and control of mostly white correctional officers. The facilities were overcrowded and dangerous. It was a familiar prison scene. Eventually, a new black prison director was brought in to "do something" (Taylor 1974).

That new director of the DC Department of Corrections was Delbert C. Jackson, who was assisted by Salanda Whitfield, administrator for Central Facility. From the beginning, the Lorton Project was bound by the provisions of the DC Department of Corrections' policies and practices governing conduct of activities at its facilities. Based upon an inmate's sentence structure, time remaining, and other criteria, the Department of Corrections recommended students for the program through its College Coordinating Committee.

Initial funding for the project was provided by Sears Roebuck Company, the Hattie Strong Foundation ($9,000), the Agnes Meyer Foundation ($10,000), Hess, Cafritz, Law Enforcement Assistance Administration (LEAA), and the Covington and Burling law firm ($5,000). The DC Department of Corrections contributed annually $48,760, which covered tuition and fees and supplied textbooks for the courses. Some students were eligible for veteran's benefits. Federal City College provided staff, faculty, and additional services as needed to ensure and maintain program quality. Various city agencies, already in partnership with DC Corrections, also participated in the seamless movement of the men through the three program phases—institutional, bussing, and internship.

Participation was always voluntary. Any student with a GED certificate or high school diploma was eligible for admission to UDC, an open admissions university, but the individual had to be recommended and agree to accept this remarkable opportunity. Higher education program directors for the DC Department of

Corrections during the twenty-seven years of the program included Dr. Wilbert Brown Jr., Gwendolyn Washington, and Alethia Hill-Simmons, all of whom added immeasurably to the success of the Lorton Project.

The underlying philosophy of the college program was to not only provide an avenue to a college degree but in the process to change the mental attitudes of the inmates, thereby reducing the chances of their recidivism or return to prison. A therapeutic model was rejected in favor of one geared more toward empowerment and purpose. Central to this process was an opportunity for the participants to engage not only in academic courses but also in the management and direction of the project itself through tutoring, student government activities, community events planning, and cultural exposure. Founder Andress Taylor, then assistant dean for community education and professor of English at Federal City College, outlined the project's four philosophical concepts: 1) development of the men as valuable human resources, 2) opportunity for the men to serve and participate in decision making, 3) community involvement, and 4) centralization and goal orientation (Taylor 1974).

It cannot be overstressed that the Lorton Project was a bold undertaking at a time when "black power" was the popular cry of the black underclass across the nation. It was a revolutionary response to recent civil rights legislation and the press for equality of opportunity. At issue was the lost manpower and talent that was decimating black communities in the District and other urban centers. Children were growing up fatherless, single female-headed households had become the norm, unemployment was rampant, and the poor saw little or no avenue for upward mobility. Dr. Thomas Stewart, now living in Oakland, California, and president of Patten University, reflected on growing up in the District:

> I do not take it for granted that I could have been one of the countless African Americans from Northeast, specifically Brentwood, who were consumed by the draconian criminal justice policies of the 80's and 90's. In fact, I am proud to demonstrate the return on investment that occurs when you educate instead of incarcerate, and I am obligated to show my gratitude by constantly paying it forward, particularly to the residents of this wonderful city. (Excerpted from a speech given at UDC on Founders' Day, February 16, 2017, Washington, DC.)

In addition to college courses, student activities involving the community were stressed as the interrelated and comprehensive structure of the program took shape. To combat the idea of just warehousing the men, many of whom were obviously capable and intelligent, it was thought that their minds needed constant stimulation and development in a more holistic approach to rehabilitation, or rather habilitation, since many of the men lacked basic positive experiences of self-management, decision making, responsibility, and cultural exposure.

The earliest classes were held at the Youth Centers and Central Facility. First, a successful pilot study was implemented in March 1969, which allowed fifty inmate volunteers to enroll in one of two sections of a course called "Introduction to Urban Social Problems," one section meeting at the Youth Center and the other at Central Facility. The men were carefully selected through an interview process with priority given to successful completion of the GED, good behavior, desire, and overall potential to succeed.

Once they applied to college and received their letter of acceptance, a whole new world opened up to them. In the college classes, the men were able to express themselves freely and to apply their own reasoning to the societal pressures they dealt with on the outside. They considered, many for the first time, issues such as welfare, taxation, poverty, ethics, and city governance. They began to discuss critically the criminal justice system of which they were a part. Many even received their social security number for the first time as a consequence of enrollment (Taylor 1974). No longer were they referred to just as convicted felons or inmates; they were now students. Subsequently, in June 1969, fifty men were allowed to take three courses each from among English, algebra, economics, and pan-African literature. These men formed the core of the institutional component of the project. Dr. Stuart Adams, assistant director for planning and research at Lorton, noted that the inmate-students found the courses "such a welcome diversion from the stultifying environment of prison life that they outperform[ed] students on the outside" (Bold, B1). Average grades were As and Bs with an average grade point average of 2.8 (Lathan B1).

The program had solid, high-level support from the outset, and the success of the endeavor became a feather in the cap of all concerned. While the university officials were concerned with curricular alignment and student outcomes, the correctional staff was concerned with institutional safety issues. The return on investment became obvious. The annual memorandum of understanding between the two District agencies was a classic example of a win-win situation and municipal cooperation.

A pre-college program was eventually started by the men themselves who emphasized values clarification. They recognized that some inmates were not ready for the rigor of the college courses. About twelve of the top students in the institutional phase served as tutors in three noncredit seminars: developmental math, problem solving, and writing. With a positive recommendation from their peers and completion of one quarter in the pre-college program, other men were allowed to enroll in courses in the project's institutional phase. The courses offered in the pre-college phase were administered by advanced students in the college program; it was the major vehicle for entrance into the program and provided leadership training for those providing the instruction.

In September 1970, the bussing component was started under strict guidelines with some of the same fifty student-inmates who were bussed from the Occoquan facility to the main Federal City College campus. This privilege or incentive had to be earned by good behavior, a common prison administrative practice. According to the PEW report, such earned time credits serve to "encourage better inmate behavior behind bars ..." (p. 25). Once the men had successfully passed the courses in the institutional phase and still had time remaining on their sentences, they became eligible for educational release or parole. They rode the bus from Occoquan to Federal City College shackled, but once on campus, they were allowed to take classes with the shackles removed to blend in with the regular students. There they had access to the university's full course offerings. The men knew that their conduct on the outside would determine the longevity of this policy, so they kept each other in compliance with the rules. They had earned the privilege of commuting to campus and did not want the opportunity to be denied because of the actions of a few.

The program founder gave some early statistics. The first twelve men were graduated in June 1973 from Federal City College. As of 1972, sixty-two men were employed; earnings were close to $400,000 with $40,000 paid in taxes. The overall grade point average of the men in the program was 2.8, the average age was twenty-seven, with an average of 2.3 dependents (Taylor, A. 1974). Word about the program spread, and some offenders began to request that the sentencing judges send them to Lorton where they could enroll in the college program.

In 1971, the internship component, called Project Start, was begun with fifteen inmates who were placed in actual work situations in the community. The transition period between release and societal adjustment was filled with job-readiness training. This paraprofessional component was first under the direction of Michael Searles and then Margaret Tyus, both committed community liaisons. Again, this was an unprecedented opportunity for only the most trusted of the inmates who had led exemplary lives on the inside and would soon be released in the community. Project Start was intended also to give the men a leg up on employment prospects upon their release. It featured a paraprofessional competitive internship that required the inmates to pass the appropriate Civil Service examination for positions at level GS 3–7. Upon graduation, these employees were eligible to apply for promotion to full professional status within the then US Department of Health, Education, and Welfare.

In many ways, Project Start was crucial to preventing recidivism. During this internship, some men were given modest support stipends from the DC Department of Vocational Rehabilitation for performing community service projects. According to the PEW study,

> Every day spent under community supervision rather than behind bars is an opportunity for a sentenced individual to work. It's an opportunity to build vocational experience, to care for children, and to pay victim restitution and other fines and fees" (pp. 24–25).

Project Start provided necessary job experience, a work ethic, time management, and positive community involvement in contrast to previous criminal involvement. It provided some students with informal leadership opportunities to serve as assistant program managers and team leaders responsible for six to ten interns and operating within the bureaucracy of the second largest federal government agency at the time (Taylor 1974).

Job-readiness training was another critical component of this interagency initiative. In addition to Federal City College and the DC Department of Corrections, other city agencies contributed to the success of the project. Upon release, some of the inmates, realizing they could be role models, formed a service fraternity to give back to the community. The students established the CREATE (Committee for Rehabilitative Efforts Attained Through Education) Free School as an alternative high school for juvenile first offenders. They also operated drug counseling and tutorial programs in area juvenile detention centers and local high schools. Many of these men had never had a job before, and they received a stipend provided by the DC Department of Vocational Rehabilitation for their community service work in CREATE. The program founder noted that "in November of 1972, CREATE organized a slate of student candidates and won control of the Federal City College Student Government" (Taylor, p. 178). By 1974, about fifty high school students had graduated through the CREATE Free School, and some of them went on to enroll at Federal City College; in all, about 80 percent of these were the progenies of the released students from Lorton.

The program, of course, was not without its problems. In 1971, the project was about to suspend its summer offerings because of a financial hiccup. The lack of funds to continue offering courses at Lorton was due to the city's money shortage affecting both DC Department of Corrections as well as Federal City College. Students protested the decision and sought a meeting with Warden Kenneth Hardy. They were reassured by Blair Ewing, head of the DC Office of Criminal Justice, that "federal funds would be available for the fall" (*Post*, E2). Upon the intervention of Senator Daniel Inouye (D-Hawaii), the city agreed to provide the $24,000 needed to hold the summer session classes (Moore, C5).

In a twenty-five-page report to LEAA, Adams, who had set up a similar program at San Quentin, called the Lorton Project "the best prison college program in the country" (Claiborne 1970, CI). The program was so successful and popular at the institution that LEAA increased its funding from $20,822 to $73,140, thereby allowing enrollment to increase from 161 to well over two hundred, about 10 percent of the Lorton Prison population at that time (Claiborne). In his report, Adams included comments from some of the inmates. One said, "It's the best thing that ever happened to me. I'm 23 and I've spent 15 years in institutions. I'm hoping this is my chance to get out and stay out." One faculty member was quoted as saying, "The men ... show much greater motivation than students at Federal City College ... The students are serious, they perform well, and they are interested in their work." Columnist William Raspberry of the *Washington Post* responded in an editorial to critics of the program: "... the recidivism rate for parolees of the FCC-Lorton project is about 5 per cent. The overall rate for local felons is closer to 70 per cent" (p. A21).

So successful was the LPCP at addressing the issues of drugs, poverty, and joblessness that in 1972 Congress agreed to make funding for the Prison College Project a part of the DC Appropriations Bill, thereby making it a part of the annual DC budget. In June 1973, the program's first twelve student-inmates graduated in four years in the on-campus ceremony along with the other graduates. Dr. Andress Taylor was named "Outstanding Educator of America" in 1973 by the national organization of the same name. At this point, according to Taylor (1974), there were 305 active students in the three phases of the program, and the recidivism rate for the project overall was less than 15 percent. In addition, sixty-two men were employed, and fifty were Project Start interns. In testament to the program's success, the US Department of Health, Education, and Welfare adopted the Lorton Project as a national model.

Also in 1973, the first annual track and field games were held. This was a program organized by the inmates themselves in which their children, other local children, family, and friends were invited to participate and watch as children won trophies and other recognition for physical accomplishments, including relay races and other track events, all supervised and operated by the inmates. Metro busses were made available to transport participants along the L90 route to the Central Facility to participate in the games and then return them back to the city in the evening.

Then, in 1974, an incident occurred in which three bussing students were caught and charged in a bank robbery while on release to attend classes on campus. This incident effectively ended the bussing component of the program.

When Alzona J. Davis took over the directorship in 1975, the Lorton Project was becoming unwieldy. Davis boosted the organizational structure of the project by hiring additional staff to focus on the academic strength of the institutional phase; the name was changed to the more formal Lorton Prison College Program. Under his leadership, the institutional phase of the program became a quasi-satellite campus. It was degree oriented, and students were able to fully matriculate from the admissions application to the final degree inside the prison walls (Pendleton 1986).

Students, now unable to come to the campus programs in the evening, held the first in-house awards ceremony at Lorton to recognize student achievement. Other organized activities followed. In 1975, the Lorton students conducted their first of several Criminal Institution Conferences. Prominent lawyers, government officials, community activists, and others served as panelists and debated issues of jurisprudence prompted by student questions and their firsthand observations of the criminal justice system. UDC Criminal Justice professor Dr. Kelsey Jones was instrumental in assisting the students to organize the conferences by making outside contacts and structuring the dialogue. For instance, on November 20, 1976, a symposium was held focusing on "How Incarceration Affects the Family" featuring keynote speaker Irv Joyner, coordinator for the Commission for Racial Justice.

1977–1995

In 1977, the first UDC graduation ceremony was held at the Lorton Central Facility with full academic protocol in effect. UDC's first president, Lisle C. Carter, officiated. The District's first black mayor, the Honorable Walter Washington, attended and addressed the graduates. The student speaker was William Biggs, who later was cited in "Who's Who in American Colleges and Universities" in 1980. By this time, enrollment in the three program phases stood at about three hundred students.

A branch of the UDC Student Government Association, Lorton Unit, was established and organized by students in the institutional phase. A primary function of the Lorton SGA was to provide residents with experiences in budgeting, program planning, parliamentary procedures, governance, and leadership. The Lorton SGA was comprised of seven departments or committees: Legal

Affairs, Student Activities, Pre-College Program, Planning and Research, Student Affairs, Community Relations, and the Student Newsletter. The student newsletter, the *People's Press,* proved to be an outlet for both creative expression and a source of information about daily events at the facilities. In one memorable instance, main campus SGA leaders met at Lorton to discuss allocation of student fees for clubs and organizations. At issue was the 1979–80 budget request of $6,000 for the SGA at Lorton to support such activities as the annual basketball tournament, a family social, a prison conference, newsletters, and the track and field meet. Initially, they had received only $2,000, but as a result of the meeting, they were able to secure another $4,000 through the school's Budget and Finance Committee (Jones).

The university project staff remained fairly consistent during these later years. Al Davis, military retiree, directed the program from 1975 until his retirement in 1990. Thelma Reddick provided administrative support as the program assistant, and Denise Kinlaw was secretary. Dr. Donald Fagon served as faculty administrator, and Malvery Henry was academic coordinator. Ernesta Pendleton replaced Robbie Beatty as program analyst in 1979; she was later appointed acting director in 1990 upon the retirement of Al Davis and remained in the position until 1994. During this period, she was called to provide expert testimony before a Congressional Black Caucus committee on Capitol Hill examining successful offender rehabilitation programs. UDC professor of urban studies Howard Croft directed the program in its remaining months.

John T. Butler replaced Michael Jackson as counseling coordinator and was succeeded by Kirby Parker. This position was actually located primarily on site at the prison and provided advising, counseling, and overall coordination of student services. Van Quarles served as project assistant, and Gloria Stokes was coordinator for the Cultural Arts Forum from 1978 to 1988. Butler would later return briefly to UDC in 2012 as the associate vice president for development. Denise Kinlaw, well regarded by the men and a product of the inner-city Shaw community, served longest on the project staff, beginning as secretary and ending as counseling coordinator in 1995 when the program ended. Kinlaw, a community worker, was known and admired for her ability to type one hundred words per minute as well as for her rapport with the students, both inside and outside the gates of Lorton.

In 1984, student enrollment in the institutional phase alone was about two hundred, and the curriculum had expanded to include degree programs in urban studies, legal assistance, business management, and accounting. In addition, students began an academic tutorial program to assist each other to pass the rigorous courses. At the Youth Centers, more young inmates were signing up to participate in their own Youth Symposium. Their motto was, "The most powerful arsenal is a mind—not a gun."

In 1989, the DC Department of Corrections, under Director Hallem Williams, built a new academic building with six classrooms, three offices, and a library. The correctional prison college administrator (Wilbert Brown) was housed there. The LPCP curriculum was expanded or modified, and computer courses were initiated. Academic emphasis was never just on rote memory of content but critical thinking as well. It was the critical thinking, questioning, and sense of debate that encouraged the men and gave them the confidence and boldness to continue their studies.

Consequently, registration was a major activity each semester. Each student was issued a UDC identification card during the first semester of enrollment, and it was required for all subsequent registrations. There was a five-dollar replacement fee assessed for lost ID cards. The program analyst, in consultation with UDC on-campus department chairs, created the class schedule each semester and summer session. Faculty assignments were approved by the various department chairs. The students looked forward to seeing what courses would be offered and which faculty member would be teaching them. They stood in line, got advisor's signatures, and registered. The UDC counselor would then take the registration materials to main campus for input into the institution's mainframe computer system (SIS+). The university calendar was observed for add/drops or withdrawals. Testing for class placement and transcript evaluations were overseen by staff from the campus University College. Again, the counselor was responsible for the logistics, seeing that the necessary paperwork was generated and processed. Textbooks were ordered, received, and signed for. Books were provided free of charge to Lorton students and distributed by the Department of Corrections as near as possible to the first class session, to be returned at the end of the semester for redistribution to the next class in some instances.

Academic advisement for students at Lorton consisted of meetings with the correctional counselor and (or) the university counselor each semester for initial programming, then as needed for ongoing advisement with the counselor or other program staff.

Class attendance sheets were monitored by both university staff and correctional staff. Students on academic probation or those experiencing attendance issues, such as disciplinary segregation, institutional movement, or illness, were priority subjects for either self-initiated counseling sessions or sessions prompted by correctional program staff. Since all staff hired in this effort were potential change agents, they had to be sensitive and committed to addressing the unique needs of the inmates. Students were expected and encouraged to adhere to appointments, activity scheduling, and class times.

A major strength of the Lorton Prison College Program was the devoted part-time adjunct faculty and full-time staff members who believed in the philosophy of the endeavor and who worked hard to provide quality services and instruction for the inmates. Faculty members were recruited from the university staff and the business community as well. The adjunct faculty pay was typical and modest ($1,200–$1,800 per course), and each adjunct left the campus or other worksite, traveled the twenty minutes along Route 95 to Virginia, subjected himself or herself to body searches to enter the facilities, and often faced less than optimal conditions and resources. These were well-qualified and trained adjunct instructors who met all of the campus requirements for hiring. Some taught at Lorton for twenty years or more, giving the program its much-needed stability and consistency. Periodic faculty meetings were held on the main campus, with the program director presiding, to address faculty and administrative concerns and to discuss such matters as absenteeism, lockdowns, and other matters affecting student progress and academic requirements. Adherence to the

Lorton Psion College Handbook as well as other university policies were discussed as warranted. Correctional staff attended as well.

Faculty members were encouraged to use their own disclosure and experiences to be live demonstrations of what could be achieved with faith and focused effort. These role models, urban educators, representing several ethnicities and various countries of origin, provided a worldview that extended well beyond the District of Columbia. Some were American, some African, some white, some East Indian, some Caribbean, and some female. They were different from the men in demeanor and expectations. And yet they were able to engage the students by reshaping mind-sets and providing alternatives to their disclosures as well. Feelings of confidence, ability, and purpose replaced doubt, confusion, and apathy. The inmate-students were impressed at the faculty knowledge being afforded them by individuals who treated them civilly and as if they mattered.

Classes were not watered down at Lorton. The students were expected and challenged to be as good as or better than students on the main campus. Faculty stressed the need to take this opportunity seriously in order to one day be able to compete in the world of work where they would have to be twice as good due to their race and criminal record. Peer support was available as well as voices of encouragement and self-disclosure. Course curricula were available in urban studies, accounting technology, computer science technology, media technology, and legal assistance.

Recognizing the developmental education structure of this academic effort, the nature and needs of incarcerated students became the focus of regular meetings where all faculty members were afforded an opportunity to exchange ideas and techniques needed for students' successful experience in the classes. Student outcomes included not only class assessments but personal efficacy outcomes as well. Upon written request, students could receive a progress report reflecting instructor evaluations, staff observations, approximate grade point average, and credit hours accumulated to date. These reports would be sent to the student, the sentencing judge, or the probation officer, as directed. A copy was kept in the student's university file. Central to the goals of the program was the belief that this higher-learning experience could reduce recidivism by instilling a more positive self-concept, thereby developing a pool of inmates who would serve as constructive role models in the prison and as they prepared for new careers as alternatives to deviant occupations upon their return to the inner city.

Among the more dedicated faculty were Professor Luther Buck (urban studies); Dr. Mohamed Elhelu (integrated science); Dr. Gregory Rigsby (English); Dr. Lewis Crenshaw (English); Dr. Paul Slepian (mathematics); Professor Charles Adams (mathematics); Professor Howard Croft (urban studies); Professor Joseph Elam (English); Dr. Thomas Oliver Jr. (English); Mr. Samuel Williams Sr. (accounting); Dr. Donald Fagon (economics); Mrs. Rosemary Fowler (English); Dr. Janet Hoston Harris (history); Ms. Judy Lyons (English); and Johnnie Landon, Esq. (legal assistance). One faculty member, Dr. Emanuel Chatman (accounting), who taught twenty years at the prison, was selected three times as "Teacher of the Year" by the student inmates.

Caribbean professor C.L.R. James, who taught Pan-African literature in the early years of the program, had an annual lecture named in his memory on the main UDC campus, the C.L.R. James Honors Convocation. At the university, C.L.R. James was Star Professor of History from 1970 to 1980, and the institution's first honorary degree, the Doctor of Humane Letters, was conferred upon Dr. James in 1980. At Lorton, the students often referred to the "C.L.R. James Chair at Lorton."

Ernesta Pendleton, program analyst and later acting director, surveyed the Lorton instructors in researching her dissertation, *Factors Influencing the Retention of Faculty Teaching Developmental Students at Military and Correctional Sites* in 1995 from Grambling State University (Louisiana). The study found that faculty in these outlying settings were motivated by intrinsic values, not money, and that their longevity in the program was due to feelings of contributing to something worthwhile, a sense of autonomy, and the support received from staff. These military- and correctional-based programs enabled the faculty to exercise compassion toward their fellow man in a supportive environment of respect and accountability. Faculty felt they had ownership in the process of changing a human being. The value added by these faculty role models cannot be overestimated. About 70 percent male, these individuals came to signify success, professionalism, and caring. At least two later became ministers, carrying out the Gospel of Christ and promoting Christian love, possibly as a result of their prison experience.

Such admiration was not one sided. Professors new to the correctional programs were always impressed at the level of questioning and critical thinking skills the students displayed. The men had a thirst for knowledge and read voraciously; often they would want to continue discussions past the class time. The education they received and the opportunity to write and express their perspectives were cathartic, life-changing experiences. As one observer posited,

> Working at class assignments gives prisoners a purpose in life and a focus. Success with completion of a course or earning a good grade can produce an understanding of the consequences of one's actions and a desire to take responsibility for them. Success in course work builds their self-esteem and helps them envision a different kind of life than that of crime. (Zoukis, p. 35)

These adult learners, though imprisoned for wrongdoing, wanted rehabilitation and redemption; they embraced education as a means to that end. Some expressed that the college experience for them replaced loneliness, idleness, and dread with a sense of hope and purpose.

Additional individuals who assisted and supported the primary program staff were various UDC administrators, trustees, and other committed advocates: Dr. Jeanne Lea (VP for Student Affairs), Dr. Betty Verbal (dean, continuing education), Mr. Leon Gurley (UDC photographer), Dr. Bobbie Austin (VP for Advancement), Rev. Walter Fauntroy (civil rights activist), UDC Trustee Dr. N. Joyce Payne and Honorable Ronald Brown, UDC Board of Trustees chairman and former US secretary of commerce, respectively.

Some colleagues on the main campus are deserving of special

mention. Mary Roberts of the UDC Office of Student Program Development was assigned to oversee the university's satellite programs. She worked with the Lorton students from the late 1970s through the early 1980s as a program development specialist to help foster student growth and development through program planning, budgeting, and negotiating techniques. Her duties included coming regularly to Lorton to assist LPCP students with their activities, including student elections, homecoming involvement, speaker's series, and fashion shows. Ms. Roberts was the outside liaison who would get the signatures of university administrators for needed transactions, receive checks, and pay vendors. Because of her assistance and diligence, the events at Lorton were well coordinated and of high quality.

Cultural Arts Forum

The institutional Distinguished Lecture Series was started in 1970 by program coordinator Gene Emanuel and featured primarily politicians, artists, and authors. These activities were aimed at the college program audience, but other selected inmates were allowed to attend as well. The name was later changed to the Cultural Arts Forum, coordinated by Gloria Odom Stokes, who brought local and national performers and other activities to the Central Facility from 1978 to 1992. The men enjoyed the quality sessions brought in for their enjoyment and development. Many times, these were enrichment activities that the men were not accustomed to and likely would not have been exposed to if they had not been incarcerated. When classical violinist Gerald Lucas played for them, they were able to relate it to a popular Grey Poupon commercial they had seen. These fora were offered on a monthly basis, sometimes bimonthly, with about fifteen to twenty-five inmates in attendance. Among the offerings were the UDC and Howard University jazz bands, acclaimed poet Gwendolyn Brooks, Grammy-Award-winning singers Sweet Honey in the Rock, poet and playwright Imamu Baraka, author Nathan Heard, relationship expert Dr. Audrey Chapman, church choirs, motivational speakers, and various career-related field experts who made presentations. The men were especially appreciative of those who took the time to come to the prison, and the presenters were impressed by the intelligence and respect shown by the men.

Commencement

Commencements at the Central Facility took place in the sweltering heat of mid to late July. Nevertheless, they were always joyous occasions with invited family, friends, and guests in attendance. The ceremonies were held in the Lorton Chapel with a reception following. Students, staff, and faculty, dressed in traditional college regalia, marched in to the sound of "Pomp and Circumstance" played by Dr. Lewis Crenshaw on a UDC organ brought annually to the facility to be tuned on site for the occasion. Musical selections frequently were performed by the Lorton gospel group, the Spiritual Kings (Rector 1978). Rev. William C. Bailey, tenor, sang "You'll Never Walk Alone" at one commencement accompanied by Audrey Jean Childs on organ. UDC photographer Leon Gurley was always on hand to create memorable pictures of the event, and local television crews and reporters provided media coverage.

Commencement speakers at Lorton were always individuals who lent appropriate gravitas to the ceremony. For example, the orator for commencement '82 was feisty New York Democratic Congresswoman Shirley Chisolm, who challenged the graduates to not look behind once they had paid their debt to society. She noted Chief Justice Warren Berger's recent address to the American Bar Association in which he opined that a man should be able to learn his way out of prison. In 1986, Congressman Mervyn Dymally (D-CA) urged the twelve graduates to use "their credentials and their credibility" to improve prison conditions and to be "in the vanguard of a national movement for prison reform." The 1987 commencement featured Dr. Arthur Thomas, president of Central State University in Wilberforce, Ohio, who challenged the graduates to "Take the degree and do something with it, but never forget where [they] came from." He shared his own early experiences growing up poor in Dayton, Ohio. He reminisced that many of his achievements in life were sparked by an early prediction that he would never amount to anything, but he was motivated and could stand before them as the president of his alma mater by his midforties.

Student speakers were impressive as well. In 1981, Robert Crowe Jr. made an impassioned plea to the audience to "tear down those fences that separate us mentally." He used the occasion to advocate for incentives for the graduates such as time reduction and education furloughs.

The ninety-minute ceremony was often emotional, given the circumstances and the obvious dedication and stamina shown by the men who successfully reached their academic goals. In addition to their degrees from the university, the DC Department of Corrections gave out awards. Graduates with a 3.0 or better grade point average received academic achievement plaques and a modest monetary grant for completing their studies with distinction. The student with the highest academic average had the honor of giving the student speech or presenting the class gift. Everyone, including the mayor, was there to shake hands and express congratulations.

Other notables who participated in commencements and on-site programs at Central Facility in addition to Honorable Shirley Chisolm, the first African American to run for US president, were Honorable Jesse Jackson Sr., president of Operation PUSH; Jim Vance, local newscaster (WRC-TV); Cathy Hughes (owner and CEO, Radio One); DC Mayors Honorable Walter Washington and Honorable Marion Barry; and DC City Council members Honorable Hilda Mason, Honorable Sterling Tucker, Honorable Harry Thomas, and Honorable Willie Hardy. The UDC presidents always officiated, and Dr. Rafael Cortada was commencement speaker in 1988 as well.

By 1990, the LPCP was stable in enrollment, but there were talks of scaling back the program in order to save money. Some corrections support positions were cut. The students successfully lobbied the District's United Black Fund under the direction of community activist Dr. Calvin Rolark for financial support, and other funds were provided as well to keep tutoring and networking projects afloat. One highlight of that year was captured in *Jet* magazine (May 21, 1990). Edward Michael Hawkins (serving time for robbery and murder), completed his baccalaureate degree in urban studies with a 4.0 grade point average, the top UDC graduate for the entire campus. He subsequently was employed through the DC Corrections Work Training Program with the National Institutes of Health (NIH) in Bethesda, Maryland, as a messenger.

In 1993, the first Andress Taylor Award (named for the founder) was presented to Arthur Scott-El. This award was given to a student who held a position of trust (student government president), possessed outstanding leadership qualities, and served the community well.

In addition to the college program, UDC also contracted to provide the vocational instruction at the prison. Under the directorship of Sandra Majid-Carter from 1991 to 1995, the Voc-Tech Program also operated in the restricted prison environment, offering certificate training in word processing / office skills, auto mechanics, dental technician (prostheses), bricklaying, electrician, printing, graphic design, and plumbing. The staff consisted of experienced union journeymen who, like the college faculty, "thought of their jobs as ministries, sent to bring truth and light and hope to the inmate population" (Carter). Carter recalls the dress codes, strict attendance, and other policies outside staff were expected to adhere to in order to ensure no violation of prison policies and procedures and support of public safety. These same individuals often provided job referrals and recommendations, thereby helping the inmates find jobs upon release from the institution. In both programs, the men were able to develop "relationships with teachers, ministers, and other visitors that would form a network of support" upon release (Malloy 2013).

But by 1994, rumors of the closing of the Lorton Program began to circulate as the Barry administration faced a fiscal shortage. In 1995, Congress created the Control Board to oversee the District of Columbia with authority over municipal spending. Some of the student inmates, especially those who were close to graduation, expressed angst and dismay not knowing exactly how they would be affected or when but knowing that the LPCP was being phased out due to "lack of funding." Corrections director Walter Ridley stepped in and prolonged the inevitable, but the program officially ended in the spring of 1996. The District's economy, of course, affected UDC as well; hundreds of faculty and staff were victims of a mandatory reduction in force. Among these was yours truly, the acting director of the LPCP.

Politically, efforts were underway to dismantle the prison altogether. By 1995, the Lorton Complex was housing approximately seven thousand inmates, 44 percent over capacity (FAS). The control board recommended turning over operation of the DC prison system to the federal government. The facilities at Lorton were underfunded, outmoded, and in "dangerous disrepair," according to reports commissioned by Congress. Responding, in addition, to community complaints of poor physical plant conditions and inadequate security measures, Senator John Warner (D-VA) and other legislators successfully introduced legislation to close the facility. With the passage in 1997 of the National Capital Revitalization and Self-Government Improvement Act, the DC Department of Corrections officially began to transfer the Lorton inmate population to other states within the jurisdiction of the Federal Bureau of Prisons and discontinued the operation of the entire Lorton Correctional Complex on December 31, 2001 (Clark

2015). DC delegate and statehood advocate Eleanor Holmes Norton later explained, "[The District] was carrying a state function that no other city in the United States carries, state prisons" (Clark). Consequently, the closing of Lorton Prison was considered a prudent, cost-saving measure for the District government.

Through all of the turmoil, the inmates remained informed and politically astute. They saw the UDC programs as economic lifelines to jobs and other resources. However, they also recognized the consequences of privatization as the nation moved to build more prisons as revenue generators. They could see the handwriting on the wall and felt trapped by a system that paid them very low wages as more and more black men arrived every day. They had noted through the years that as some left, others quickly filled the void. There were generations at Lorton: fathers and sons, brothers, uncles, cousins, neighbors. At Occoquan in the middle of a hot summer day, the sight of a virtual sea of idle black men, all shapes and sizes, in the prime of their lives (ages twenty to fifty-five) was both devastating and unforgettable. Now, they were being dispersed throughout the country to complete their sentences away from family, friends—and the Lorton Prison College Program.

References

Bold, D.R. 1969. "50 Lorton Prisoners Enroll in College: Freshmen Study Behind Bars." *Washington Post,* B1, March 19.

Carter, S.M. 2013. Interview. July 2.

Claiborne, W.L. 1970. "U.S. Triples College Aid to Lorton." *Washington Post,* C1, July 22.

Clark, A. 2015. "Will D.C. Be the First U.S. City to Escape the Prison Trap?" *Next City,* September 28. Retrieved from https://nextcity.org/features/view/dc-escape-prison-trap-reentry-office-of-returning-citizens-affairs.

1971. "Ex-Prisoners Seek Funds for Lorton College Program." *Washington Post,* E2, April 1.

FAS Intelligence Resource Program. Lorton Correctional Complex. Retrieved from http://www.fas.org/irp/imint/lorton.htm.

1990. *Jet* magazine, May 21.

Jones, C.C. February 8, 1980. "Lorton, Campus SGAs Meet." *Trident* 2 (3): 1.

Lathan, A. 1970. "Lorton Inmates Doing Well in College-Level Courses." *Washington Post,* October 11.

Malloy, C. 2013. "Ex-Convict And Metrobus Driver Sidney Davis Looks to Give Something Back to D.C." *Washington Post,* March 5.

Moore, I. 1971. "College at Lorton to Go On." *Washington Post,* C5, April 2.

Pendleton, E.P. October 1986. "UDC Prison Project—An Unheralded Success." *Correctional Education Association Newsletter* 5.

Pendleton, E.P. 1995. "Factors Influencing the Retention of Faculty Teaching Developmental Students at Military and Correctional Sites." Grambling State University. Dissertation.

Raspberry, W. 1970. "Best of Blacks May Be in Jail." *Washington Post*, A21, December 15.

Rector, D. February 8, 1978. "Graduation Ceremony at Lorton." *UDC Trident* 2 (3): 1. Stewart. February 2017.

Taylor, A. Spring 1974. "Beyond Rehabilitation: The Federal City College Lorton Project—A Model Prison Higher Education Program," *Journal of Negro Education* 43 (2): 172–178.

The PEW Charitable Trusts. 2010. *Collateral Costs: Incarceration's Effect on Economic Mobility.* Washington, DC: The PEW Charitable Trusts.

Zoukis, C. 2014. *College for Convicts: The Case for Higher Education in America's Prisons.* Jefferson, NC: McFarland & Company, Inc.

Chapter 5

The Aftermath

The statistical results for inmates who earn associate and baccalaureate degrees behind bars suggest that recidivism rates are lowered considerably among this sector of the inmate population. Programs offering higher education in prison do work:

> Studies show that higher education improves cognitive function [and helps] to diminish the antisocial attitudes and behaviors associated with criminal activity. Many prisoners have credited education with ... their ability to disengage from a 'prison mentality,' maintain positive goals, and develop ... the ability to shape and steer one's life in a meaningful way. (Zoukis 2014, p. 31)

Graduates of the Lorton Prison College Program make up an invisible cadre. In most instances, they have merged back into the general population almost without notice. And perhaps this is as it should be. An individual should be able to complete his sentence and return to the community whole and functioning as any other citizen.

Over 50 percent of today's prison population is composed of black and brown men, and while some college programs have reemerged recently in some areas, there is still room for growth across the country. Washington, DC, the nation's capital, offers its UDC community college as a viable path to higher education today for those returning from prison, but no formal targeted program exists. Some isolated courses are offered online and at the DC Jail, but sentences are generally not long enough for extensive college-level programming there.

Today, the government's complicity in mass incarceration is apparent when one considers instances of failing schools, prison privatization, and gentrification. The first national challenge facing policymakers is to acknowledge the connection between lack of education on one hand and unemployment, missed opportunities, and criminal activity on the other. We've all heard the saying that "an idle mind is the devil's workshop," yet we allow schools to suspend students for minor infractions, which lead to greater transgressions. As a result of lowered high school graduation rates, we see scores of young black and Latino males unable to attend college, ineligible for the military, and unable to find meaningful employment in a nation of plenty. Inner-city schools are fraught with ineffective teachers, truant students, uninvolved parents, inadequate budgets, and low morale. Other avenues for training and personal development need to become available for those not suitable for military involvement. State and federal policymakers should consider first how to improve the urban educational system in order that it is not a pipeline to prison.

The second national challenge facing policymakers is to remove politics from the equation of determining who goes to prison, whether through sentencing guidelines, police tactics, or other means. The American power structure seems to orchestrate the course of people's lives and marginalizes their very existence in order for corporations to make huge profits. Conservative lawmakers, many of whom are holdovers from the era of segregation, continue to find ways to suppress the black male. According to Penniman (2012), who compares the current system to something you would find in a Soviet country, "The private prison companies that comprise this new American Gulag ... have a clear economic incentive to maintain the status quo" (n.p.). The American dream includes the possibility that one can rise above environmental or social circumstances. But if the deck is stacked against a specific segment of the population, that dream of opportunity becomes a nightmare of frustration and disappointment. Further, as Wiggins (2012) has noted,

> The fact that failing school systems lead to higher incarceration rates is widely known by many. And given the number of businesses profiting off of prison labor production, it seems as if certain members of society are being targeted to turn profits for large companies." (p. ?)

Those targeted, black and Latino men, make up over 50 percent of America's prison population but only 15 percent of the country's general population (Spycher et al. 2010).

The third national challenge is to eliminate poverty, homelessness, and mental illness, circumstances that give rise to the continued suppression of an identifiable segment of the population. Housing becomes a mechanism for social engineering when inner cities are redeveloped with expensive business and housing units, displacing longtime residents who can no longer afford to live in the area. When President Reagan closed the mental hospitals in the 1980s, this too had an effect on the rise in the prison population. Until mental illness and drug abuse are given the same priority as physical ailments, the prisons will continue to swell as warehousing takes the place of true rehabilitation. In the name of progress, however, it seems that more attention is being paid to the environment than to those who inhabit the space.

Historically Black Colleges and Universities (HBCUs)

American higher education is at a crossroads. President Obama has issued a challenge for the nation to regain our number-one status for worldwide college completion by 2020. Each historically black college or university has been given a specific number of additional college graduates needed to proportionately help meet this goal. These colleges and universities are uniquely suited to take on the challenge of providing programs of academic enrichment for black males.

The nation's historically black colleges and universities (HBCUs) are ideal vehicles for ensuring that low-income African American and Latino males are afforded an opportunity to become productive, learned members of society. Higher education has always been recognized as the path to upward mobility, yet funding through scholarships and grants is not sufficient to meet the needs of this population. It is unconscionable that in 2016 on the one hand, minorities are turned away from or drop out of college every day due to an inability to pay, while on the other hand, thousands are locked in a system of exploitation that makes them unavailable for college. This is lost manpower, human talent, and resources that this country can ill afford to lose in our effort to regain our standing in the world as the most well-educated citizenry. HBCUs have proven their ability to educate low-income, disadvantaged students.

The national imperative facing our legislators is how to improve foundationally our intellectual capacity, and this can be done through initiatives like the Head Start programs, TRIO, Upward Bound, college programs in prison, Black Male Achievement programs, and other targeted approaches to retrieve and rescue the black and brown male population from the cradle to prison pipeline. Efforts are needed at every level of education in order for college completion to become a reality.

Retention studies show that one of the greatest predictors of college completion is active student engagement. This matter is especially true of the black male. Harper and Quayle (2009) note that "[Black male] Students who are actively engaged in educationally purposeful activities and experiences, both inside and outside the classroom, are more likely than are their disengaged peers to persist through graduation" (p. 4). This observation, along with concurrence from stalwarts in the field of higher education (Vincent Tinto, Ernest Pascarella, Patrick Terenzini, Alexander Astin, and others) shows the strength and philosophical underpinning of the LPCP approach. At every stage in the process, students were engaged and held accountable by their professors, peers, and others.

Currently, the college graduation rate for men of color is stagnant (Harper 2012). College retention and completion rates among this group have not kept pace with other identifiable student populations. New data-driven services and approaches are needed to improve the academic experiences of this group. Male initiatives are being offered to strengthen the persistence and success of this population through such activities as workshops, mentoring programs, advisement, internship/job-readiness counseling, and other approaches. Some programs are functioning inside of prison, but most are campus- or community-based activities outside of the prison setting. Reentry services for ex-offenders are burgeoning across the country to address this issue of engagement.

Several HBCUs are accepting the challenge. Virginia Union University has announced the first Inside-Out Prison Exchange program in the state. Modeled after the nationally recognized Temple University program of the same name, this initiative offers coed classes at the City of Richmond Jail for both inmates and criminal justice majors to explore various social issues together in a classroom setting. Shaw University (NC) continues to provide an outreach prison education initiative through its Upward Bound program.

Fayetteville State University (NC) has established the Bronco MILE (Male Initiative on Leadership and Excellence) program, which challenges a group of African American male students to "lead together, to grow together, and to graduate together." This initiative is patterned after a similar program at Morgan State University (MD), which grew to five hundred members over a period of four years (*JBHE* 2012). These programs stress leadership and excellence.

Other HBCUs are sponsoring various initiatives. The University of Maryland Easter Shore's program is named Men Achieving Dreams through Excellence (MADE), and North Carolina Central University has a Centennial Scholars program for this population. These schools are taking a case-management approach that gives individual attention to students with wraparound services to address both their academic and personal concerns.

Other mainstream institutions are responding as well. For example, Albany State University's Center for the African American Male (CAAM) offers workshops, seminars, and conferences to address academic issues facing college students. In addition, partnership agreements with Upward Bound, Boys and Girls Clubs, and other community and civic organizations serve as points of contact for their mentoring and tutoring activities, including a homework hotline. Structured weekly programs are offered to strengthen persistence and leadership development opportunities.

In 2010, the overall US population declined for the first time in forty years, causing several state prisons to close, ten in Virginia alone. But this decline in the general population does not forecast a decline in the prison population as private companies such as CCA and GPO are eager to fill the gap. With proper funding to target this segment of the population, opportunities offered through HBCUs and other institutions could turn this situation around.

The nation's community colleges are also poised to provide

inmates access to college courses, and many are already involved in online and distance courses for prisoners. These institutions have a mission to offer community educational programs that will easily transition into jobs or further postsecondary programming, so the prison pipeline is within their mission to affect. But along with serving as the gateway to college, they must provide the activities and attractions to fully engage this population. Programs aimed at providing services to the families of the incarcerated are also needed to break the cycle of intergenerational dysfunction and limitations. Community college workforce development programs offer training and a supportive environment to move an individual from skills development to job readiness to gainful employment based on the needs of the local economy. Programs of higher learning are needed alongside the vocational training for that segment of the offender population that is capable and motivated. Racial and economic disparities are entrenched in American society, and only a multifaceted approach will make a lasting difference.

References

Harper, S.R. 2012. "Black Male Student Success in Higher Education: A Report from the Male College Achievement Study." Philadelphia: University of Pennsylvania, Center for the Study of Race and Equity in Education.

Harper, S. R. and Quayle, S.J. 2009. *Student Engagement in Higher Education: Theoretical Perspectives and Practical Approaches for Diverse Populations.* Routledge.

http://www.jbhe.com/2012/04/fayetteville-state-university-seeks-to-boost-retention- and-graduation-rates-of-black-men.

Penniman, N. 2012. "America's Gulag: The Money (in Politics) behind Prison Privatization." *Huffington Post* (Editorial). February 15.

Spycher, D.M., Shkodriani, G.M. and Lee, J.B. 2010. *The Other Pipeline: From Prison to Diploma.* JBL Associates, Inc.

The PEW Charitable Trusts. 2010. *Collateral Costs: Incarceration's Effect on Economic Mobility.* Washington, DC: The PEW Charitable Trusts.

Wiggins, T. February 15, 2012. "HBCUs Pose Threat to American Prison Industrial Complex." *HBCU Digest.* (Editorial).

Chapter 6

The Swan Song

The nation's capital land grant HBCU, having roots that date back to 1851 with the founding of a Normal School for Girls, UDC has no systematic outreach to its prison college alumni. No follow-up study has been done to determine the real outcome of the Lorton Project except for anecdotal recollections and the occasional reemergence of some of the men. However, studies show that inmates who earn college credits or a degree while incarcerated have a significantly lower chance of returning to prison on new charges (Zoukis 2014; Esperian 2010).

One notable LPCP graduate, Edwin Hawkins, the 4.0 valedictorian who came from a respectable, middle-class family, died of a drug overdose about seven years after release. Another honor student, Anthony "Bucky" Brown, was known to have committed suicide a few years after his release. Several others have been released and are barely thriving, but they are surviving and remaining out of prison. Still others are gainfully employed and doing quite well, raising children and being husbands. A few are known to be recidivists.

During the twenty-seven years of the program's existence, the students at Lorton were given tools to fashion a different lifestyle for themselves in order to break the cycle of crime, arrest, and incarceration. Utilizing concepts of self-awareness, education, mentoring, and community involvement, the LPCP was able to change the mental attitudes of many of these men and reduce significantly the odds of their return to prison once released. Those who took advantage of the program and were able to earn a degree benefitted most from their academic experience.

Sidney Davis, for instance, who inspired the writing of this book with his persistence, was once referred to as "a model prisoner," an inmate who had done more than any other to make good use of his time in the penitentiary (Wolfe, B1). Saddled with a lengthy sentence, Davis grabbed hold of every chance to turn his life around. He became a born-again Christian who successfully used his leadership skills to mentor and challenge other inmates to use their prison time wisely. Davis's accomplishments include a bachelor's degree from UDC in urban studies. In addition, while at Lorton he coordinated senior citizens' programs, founded the Lorton Special Olympics program, and designed and promoted drug awareness programs for other inmates as well as DC public school students (Wolfe). Today, he is gainfully employed and trying to steer youngsters toward education and away from involvement in the criminal justice system of which he was a part (Malloy 2013).

Another notable graduate of the program, James Jenkins, credits the Lorton Program for his "miraculous transformation." In correspondence, he acknowledged that the program was "the turning point in [his] life for better things" (July 11, 1916). He continued, "It was the bridge that transformed me from a hopeless drug addict content to get high until I die no matter the cost to myself or others, to a young man confident in his abilities to live a better life and determined to help others do the same." Jenkins, who earned the associate and baccalaureate degrees at Lorton, was valedictorian at his commencement. After successful government employment where he created a pilot program called Employment Opportunities for Ex-Offenders, he went on to complete a master's degree in ministry and a doctorate of divinity, with a concentration in pastoral care. Today he is an associate pastor at a local church and a special consultant at an area college.

From another perspective, however, Cedric Gilliam, who received two bachelor's degrees, one in business management and another in urban studies, paints a different picture. In a Pulitzer Prize-winning work by *Wall Street Journal* staff writer Ron Suskind, Gilliam is a minor character in the life of his son Cedric Jennings, who is the subject of the national best seller, *A Hope in the Unseen* (1998). Gilliam appears in and out of the story, which documents his journey in and out of Lorton from the age of eighteen when he received a sentence of twelve to thirty years. Released several times, Gilliam had several parole violations due to his inability to break the drug habit, even after completing a drug treatment program. When Lorton closed, he was sent to a minimum-security facility and with good behavior was eligible for parole in 2005.

Most jobs of the twenty-first century will require some degree of postsecondary education and training. As Blumenstyk (2015) notes, "By 2020, according to experts, two-thirds of all jobs will require at least some education and training beyond high school (verses

28 percent of jobs forty years ago)" (p. 3). Computer technology, cyber security, accounting, engineering, and other technical fields where jobs are plentiful will depend on an educated workforce more than ever before. The changing American economy should make room for those returning to changed environments that have established new skill requirements. As the founder of the Lorton Project noted in 1974, and it still applies today, "… somehow, with limited power and even more limited means, we must intervene in the criminal justice system to extricate from it our young manhood which is caught in the vicious cycle of arrest and release only to be re-arrested" (Taylor, A., p. 174).

What have we learned from the Lorton Prison College Program? As business mogul Oprah Winfrey would say, there are a few things we know for sure. We know that for a significant segment of the prison population, true rehabilitation is not only possible but likely, if inmates are given the resources and opportunity to thrive. The men of the Lorton higher education program were intelligent, capable, and determined to improve. Studies have shown that "offenders who participated in prison education programs were 29 percent less likely to be re-incarcerated than non-participants" (PEW, p. 23). A report by the Institute for Higher Education Policy (2005) found that recidivism among participants in college classes was 46 percent lower than for those who had not taken college classes. Zoukis (2014) cites the following: "For prisoners who attain an associate's degree: 13.7 percent recidivism; For prisoners who attain a bachelor's degree: only 5.6 percent recidivism; and For prisoners who attain a master's degree: 0 percent recidivism" (p. 13).

We know that principles of self-management lie at the heart

of a changed individual. Through interventions that promote personal emotional growth, lives and values can be altered. Time-management skills and respect for self and others make a difference in personal efficacy. The Lorton Program allowed the participants to support and respect each other in a somewhat emotionally safe environment. The men were then free to correct and explore spiritual values and concepts that inspired change. The LPCP sought to affirm the dignity and worth of human life, but we as a society must also educate the public to accept these changed individuals and give them the chance to grow and excel without undue stigma.

We know that many inmates want an avenue for restitution and reentry to the community with full acceptance, as evidenced through restored voting rights and job eligibility. Recent efforts have led several states to allow ex-offenders to vote once they are released. Others allow voting once the ex-offender is off of parole or probation. The concept of redemption or restorative justice should be fully considered. According to Blumstein and Nakamura (2009), "Currently, employers have no empirical guidance on when it might be considered safe to overlook a past criminal record when hiring an ex-offender for a particular job."(n.p.) At some point in time, an ex-offender should be able to reach a point where his past mistakes are no longer used against him. The men of the Lorton Program were taught how to make meaningful contributions for their own uplift as well as that of their communities.

We know that the current restrictions placed on ex-offenders do harm, not only to the ex-offender but to others as well and that the collateral damage done by the prison experience is way and above the punishment that is necessary for one person's correction. Voting, education, the ability to get a job, licensing, and other challenges facing the ex-offender do damage to family stability and take away the very hallmarks of citizenship (Western 2006).

We know that "There is a direct correlation between communities with high incarceration rates and low performing schools. If we invested more in education, we would need less for prisons" (Zoukis 2014). Unfortunately, this logic escapes the average citizen who falls for the universal stereotype of the inmate as incorrigible and undeserving of higher education. But policymakers who understand this economic reality must be bold and steadfast in their support of cost-effective correctional education at all levels and advocate for its sustainability. Urban educators should advance policies that take into consideration the need for targeted resources to support schools serving this population at every level.

We know that there is a better way than incarceration to treat drug addiction and abuse. In 2000, the Drug Policy Alliance was formed. This nonprofit advocacy group is the leading national organization dedicated to ending the war on drugs by working to change legislation by developing policies and regulations that are more humane and data driven. Also, spearheaded by ten bipartisan senators, the Sentencing Reform and Corrections Act is before Congress. This act would reduce mandatory minimum sentences and grant more judicial discretion, among other reforms. Thus, the drug disparities have reached concern at the highest levels of government, and changes are expected to be implemented soon to treat nonviolent drug abuse primarily as a health issue, not a crime issue.

And if we know nothing else, we know that there is a better way to promote family values. Separation of the black man from his family for extended periods breeds alienation, distrust, and family dysfunction. Correctional education programs offer a way of bridging the gap toward reunification. Qualitatively,

> ... many studies demonstrate that postsecondary prison education programs offer a chance to break the intergenerational cycle of inequality. When children are inspired by their parents to take education more seriously, they too begin to see viable alternatives to dropping out of school and entering a life of crime, thus breaking a harrowing cycle of intergenerational incarceration. (Why Prison Education?, n.p.).

Programs of retributive justice even at the junior high and high school levels would help to promote the idea of education and reflection as deterrents to criminal behavior. If we can replace the correctional approach of punishment with one of rehabilitation, then surely the postsecondary education route promises more success for reduced recidivism. As J.M. Taylor (2006) concludes, "the prison college graduate more than pays for his incarceration and education just through taxation, not to mention law abiding behavior as opposed to the norm of continued criminality" (p. 5). It is this sense of unlocked potential that resonates through each prison education program.

Historically, America has stood for fairness and equality of opportunity, recognizing the right of every individual to be free to pursue his or her dreams and goals. Surely in the twenty-first century we are not reverting back to the philosophy of chattel slavery, yet the ex-offender is stigmatized and treated as a nonentity. Evidence of second-class citizenship for the ex-offender is spelled out in several ways. In 1996, President Clinton signed the Personal Responsibility and Work Opportunity Reconciliation Act, placing a five-year lifetime limit on Temporary Assistance to Needy Families (TANF). The bill also banned anyone with a felony conviction from receiving welfare or food stamps; hence, public housing projects can exclude ex-offenders from obtaining a place to live. In addition, thirty-one states practice lifetime exclusion from jury service by ex-offenders, garnishment of paychecks for child support, and deny ex-felons the right to vote (Heitzeg 2010). In short,

> ... the stigma of having a felony record can be an insurmountable obstacle when a former inmate is eligible for employment. Job seekers with a criminal record are offered half as many positions as those without criminal records, and African American applicants receive two-thirds fewer offers. (PEW, p. 22)

It seems easy in these instances to blame the victims (ex-offenders), but as Frederick Douglass has been attributed as saying, "It is much easier to build strong children than to repair broken men."

The drug epidemic and its attendant war has been a failure of major proportions. The drugs are still plentiful, urban areas are filled with the resulting violence and crime, and the economy is such that unemployment is rampant. In order to reverse this untenable state of entropy, public policies must be reexamined and changed. Our priorities must be rethought: money spent for mass incarceration should be redirected to education and programs of retributive justice in order to strengthen our communities, not continue to tear them down.

The District's black and brown youngsters are not expendable. Schools and communities must become more responsible for establishing discipline, high expectations, and increased time on task for male students. It is no longer acceptable to lose generations of male youngsters to a system that targets these citizens by deciding that society cannot or will not make a way for their continued growth and development. Currently, black and brown men make up over half of the prison population in this country, which is nothing short of a national disgrace. Today, DC inmates are housed in one hundred different federal prisons located throughout the country, with many of them in facilities at least five hundred miles from home (Moyer 2013, p. B3). Familial relationships are difficult to maintain even under the best of circumstances and even more so when limited contact is involved.

Fortunately, public sentiment at last is swinging back in favor of rehabilitation for ex-offenders. Programs and resources are being made available in large measure as a result of political pressures in an election period. More citizens are speaking out concerning the structural inequalities in the American society as well as the need for various sentencing reforms and systemic changes. Injustices that grew out of the war on drugs are being recognized, and some activists are calling for an end to the drug war that has been so ineffective as to have done probably more harm than good. Systemic barriers to employment, housing, and voting are receiving renewed attention, and efforts are underway to lessen the ex-offender stigma, especially for nonviolent crimes.

To erase the prison stigma, community outreach and programs of inclusion must become the cornerstones of social policies for ex-offender reentry. In a recent poignant letter to President Barack Obama, hip-hop mogul Russell Simmons challenged the president to end the war on drugs, establish job-training programs, and promote an affordable education system in order to rebuild families and communities across America (*The Black Blog*, Nov. 26, 2012). Much to his credit, in February 2014, the president announced his My Brother's Keeper Initiative, a $200M national program to encourage private industry to create more opportunities for young men of color. He called on employers and the business community in general to open doors of employment and mentorship for this segment of the population. Attention must be paid to "the least of these," many of whose ancestors built this country into the powerhouse it is today. We can begin to heal the nation by strengthening educational programming for black and brown urban youth and implementing practical solutions to solve this national issue. In addition, we must embrace correctional education fully, which will inspire those captive to set themselves on a course of true rehabilitation. As Blumstein and Nakamura (2009) conclude, age and time clean should be factored in when considering an ex-offender's job readiness.

In 2015, in an unprecedented move, President Obama,

working with the Justice Department, signed a bill that reduces the unequal sentencing for crack as opposed to powder cocaine. As a part of this systemic change in criminal justice policy, he also approved the release of over six thousand inmates across the country who fall under the new guidelines for having served enough time for nonviolent drug offenses. This act, referred to as the Clemency Project 2014, will undoubtedly be a highlight of his administration.

Third, he committed funds to establish a My Brother's Keeper (MBK) Task Force, an advisory group charged with examining public policies and recommending changes needed to advance the condition of minority youth and young men of color in America. At the heart of the MBK initiative is the establishment of state and local community challenge programs with federal guidance that are focused on alleviating violence, school discipline issues, chronic absenteeism, job scarcity, and lack of mentoring. MBK is focused on six milestones:

- getting a healthy start and entering school ready to learn
- reading at grade level by third grade
- graduating from high school ready for college and career
- completing postsecondary education or training
- successfully entering the workforce
- keeping kids on track and giving them second chances

Various mentoring initiatives and male empowerment symposia are being held throughout the country's inner cities. Included, and hopefully not as an afterthought, is the need for second-chance solutions and a reconsideration of Pell Grants for prisoners. Allowing the use of Pell Grants for prisoners again would usher in a renewed era of higher education for the nation's incarcerated citizens.

Again, the District of Columbia has become a pioneer in helping to recognize and solve these urban issues. With as many as eight thousand ex-offenders returning to the District each year, the DC Department of Corrections is now focused on providing meaningful municipal services to its citizens (Clark 2015). Washington, DC has launched a two-pronged attack to address postprison reintegration and, ultimately, citizenship. First, the city has completely removed voting restrictions for released felons, including those on parole or probation. This act means that voting privileges have been restored as well.

Moreover, the Office on Returning Citizens Affairs (ORCA) was founded in 2008 as a legally mandated one-stop agency to provide wraparound ex-offender services through cooperative arrangements with the Office on Aging, the Department of Employment Services, and other District agencies. Once again, the District is ideal for testing a model program, the success of which has national implications. Completely free and voluntary, ORCA is an agency that the city can look to for advice, direction, and follow-up, but more funding and resources are needed to ensure citizen needs are assessed and addressed even prior to leaving prison.

These approaches signal that another era of prison reform is upon us. A critical look at incarceration is needed before, during, and after the fact, to address the many challenges presented by the current pipeline strategy that clearly is not working to reduce crime. There must be a way to deter violence, reduce excessive sentencing, and allow an individual to leave prison morally strong, more willing to work, and more purposefully driven to thrive.

References

Blumenstyk, G. 2015. *American Higher Education in Crisis: What Everyone Needs to Know.* Oxford University Press: New York.

Blumstein, A. and Nakamura, K. June 2009. "'Redemption' in an Era of Widespread Criminal Background Checks." National Institute of Justice. No. 263.

Clark, A. 2015. "Will D.C. Be the First U.S. City to Escape the Prison Trap?" *Next City.* Retrieved from https://nextcity. org/features/view/dc-escapr-prison-trap-reentry-office-of-returning-citizens-affairs.

Erisman, W. and Contardo, J.B. 2005. "Learning to Reduce Recidivism." Institute for Higher Education Policy.

Jenkins, J.N. Correspondence, July 11, 2016.

Malloy, C. 2013. "Ex-Convict and Metrobus Driver Sidney Davis Looks to Give Something Back to D.C. *Washington Post,* March 5.

Moyer, J. 2013. "Corrections Council Setting Pace." *Washington Post,* B3, January 22.

Simmons, R. 2012. The Black Blog. *Open Letter.* Nov. 26.

Suskind, R. 1998. *A Hope in the Unseen: An American Odyssey from the Inner City to the Ivy League.* New York: Broadway Books.

Taylor, A. Spring 1974. "Beyond Rehabilitation: The Federal City College Lorton Project—A Model Prison Higher Educatio88n Program. *Journal of Negro Education* 43 (2): 172–178.

Taylor, J.M. 2006. "Pell Grants for Prisoners Part Deux: It's Déjà Vu All over Again." *Journal of Prisoners on Prisons,* Online version.

The PEW Charitable Trusts. 2010. *Collateral Costs: Incarceration's Effect on Economic Mobility.* Washington, DC: The PEW Charitable Trusts.

Western, B. 2006. *Punishment and Inequality in America.* New York: Russell Sage Foundation.

"Why Prison Education?: The Higher The Degree, The Lower The Recidivism Rate." Retrieved from http://prisonstudiesproject.org/why-prison-education-programs/.

Wolfe, F. "Inmate-Students at Lorton Decry Possible UDC Cuts." *Washington Times,* B1–B2.

Zoukis, C. 2014. *College for Convicts: The Case for Higher Education in American Prisons.* Jefferson, NC: McFarland & Company, Inc.

Epilogue

The closing of the Lorton Correctional Facilities was long in discussion. Central to the conversation was what to do with the inmates and what would happen to the land. In 1998, Congress passed the Lorton Technical Corrections Act with instructions to maximize the use of the land for parks, recreation, and open space. By 2001, all inmates had been distributed and relocated to other federal facilities throughout the country and Lorton Prison had been closed. In 2002, the land reverted back to Fairfax City, Virginia, for redevelopment.

The acreage that once housed the Lorton Prison complex is today known as Laurel Hill. Some of the remaining buildings that have historic value will likely be preserved. But with the addition of housing, trails, a golf course, an arts center, and other amenities, the area has quietly made its transformation into a modern, upscale, desirable destination. Housing includes single-family dwellings as well as apartments, condos, and half-million-dollar townhouses. Along with the housing comes a new high school as well as shopping complexes with stores and restaurants catering to a middle-class clientele. According to one observer,

Today, you can drive down Lorton Road and never know that the rolling hills of the surrounding countryside were once part of the now-defunct prison farm, or that the two-lane brick bridges you pass along the way were built by Lorton inmates more than 40 years ago. (Shin 2001)

Time and progress march on.

Most, if not all, of the men from Lorton will likely return someday to Washington, DC, but they will find a city changed in many ways. DC is no longer a sleepy, southern town as some have called it. The complexion of the city has changed, and it is in the process of becoming, for better or worse, as promised, "One City, One Future." The new mayor, the Honorable Muriel Bowser, has continued the development projects transforming the cityscape. Vigorous development, including new retail stores and restaurants, improved streets and city services, expensive housing, and charter schools are attracting young white residents in large numbers. In a recent *Washington Examiner* article, Connolly (2012) notes the shifting population patterns:

> Whites now make up 34 percent of D.C.'s residents— up from less than 28 percent in 1999—while the black population has dropped from 60 percent to 51 percent over the same period … median household income has climbed 14 percent to $61,835 … (n.p.)

The health and vitality of the nation's capital to outward appearances belies the underbelly that continues to struggle as "progress" is made.

Today, UDC is flourishing under the leadership of President Ronald Mason Jr. Having recently received a full ten-year accreditation from the Middle States Accrediting Association with eleven out of fourteen commendations, the institution is stretching its muscles as it embraces its Vision 20/20 initiative to become a globally recognized advanced public system of higher learning, celebrating green spaces and increased enrollment. New branding ideas have shaped a brighter future for the once-beleaguered institution.

The District government under Mayor Bowser's leadership is tackling statehood and, among others things, the opening of the first all-male high school, the Ron Brown College Preparatory High School. Nationally, the Black Lives Matter coalition is focusing attention on the need for police procedures that reflect basic standards of decency in the treatment of all citizens, especially black and Latino males in the inner cities. The moral imperative is strong for criminal justice/prison reform, because social justice in America is far from perfect, but as Dr. Martin Luther King Jr. proclaimed in an address to the Southern Christian Leadership Conference on August 16, 1967, "The arc of the moral universe is long, but it bends toward justice."

References

Connolly, M. 2012. "District Grows Whiter as Suburbs Grow More Diverse." *Washington Examiner,* December 6.

Shin, A. 2001. "Ten Things to Do Before Closing a Prison." *Washington City Paper,* March 9.

Index

U

University of the District of
     Columbia – 38-39

V

Verbal, Betty – 57
Vocational/Technical Program – 61

W

Walnut Street Jail – 18
War on Drugs – 24-25
Washington, Gwendolyn – 41
Washington, Walter – 60
White-El, Matthew – 53
Whitfield, Salanda – 40
Williams, Hallem – 53
Williams, Samuel – 61
Winfrey, Oprah – 78

Y

Youth Center – 15, 43, 53